THE 10 COMMANDMENTS OF
parenting

THE 10 COMMANDMENTS OF
parenting

The Do's and Don'ts for Raising Great Kids

ED YOUNG

MOODY PUBLISHERS
CHICAGO

All Scripture quotations, unless otherwise indicated, are taken from the *New American Standard Bible®*, Copyright © The Lockman Foundation 1960, 1962, 1963, 1968, 1971, 1972, 1973, 1975, 1977, 1995. Used by permission.

Scripture quotations marked NIV are taken from the *Holy Bible, New International Version®*. NIV®. Copyright © 1973, 1978, 1984 by International Bible Society. Used by permission of Zondervan Publishing House. All rights reserved.

Scripture quotations marked KJV are taken from the King James Version.

Library of Congress Cataloging-in-Publication Data

Young, H. Edwin, 1936-
    The 10 commandments of parenting : the do's and don'ts for raising great kids / by Ed Young.
        p. cm.
    ISBN 0-8024-3147-X
    1. Parenting—Religious aspects—Christianity. I. Title.

BV4526.3.Y68 2004
248.8'45—dc22

2003022654

1 3 5 7 9 10 8 6 4 2

Printed in the United States of America

In memory of Jo Beth's and my parents,
Katherine and G. B. Landrum and
J. L. E. and Homer Young.
We are the product of their selfless love,
sacrifice, and devotion.

And to
Ed and Lisa, Ben and Elliott, and Cliff and Danielle.
You're doing a great job parenting our grandchildren,
LeeBeth, E. J., Laurie, Landra, Nicole,
Claire, Rachel, and Susannah.

CONTENTS

PREFACE:
PARENTING—AN
OVERWHELMING "CALLING"

The early response of neophyte moms and dads is much the same—"I had no idea!"

If you only have been a child and never a parent, in all probability you are dogmatic about the role. I had all the answers until God blessed me with "the calling." Suddenly the stock of my parents went up, and through the years it continued to climb. This is the usual pattern.

Meanwhile, back in the family, every parent needs sage-like wisdom to train up a child in the way God has bent him or her (note Proverbs 22:6). To discern the bent and to encourage the bent—that's the challenge. Dads and moms of the twenty-first century would call a parenting hotline daily if that service were available.

"The calling" is overwhelming and unending. I know. I've been there and done that, and with three grown sons and three "daughters-in-love" and eight grandchildren, "the calling" continues.

People regularly ask for advice and tips for their "911" parenting dilemmas. I normally offer an assuring word and open up my parenting first aid kit and hand out a Band-Aid or two. My real temptation (when time permits) is to over-answer the question with obscure theological profundities. A quick fix by definition is a quick fix—it doesn't last. Theological profundities without practical application shirk the issues.

The 10 Commandments of Parenting lays a biblical foundation for parenting. My goal is to make it clear, keep it simple, and let it sing. In the process I share some of the mountaintops and valleys Jo Beth and I have traversed with our sons.

Many times we missed the moment to communicate. All too often we disciplined inappropriately. I made many mistakes, misjudgments, and poor decisions with my kids. It's a miracle they are solid Christian husbands and parents. Thank you, Lord.

I can say from personal experience that God superintends "the calling" when we humbly seek Him and get most of it right. We model and mold. We love and encourage. We talk a little and listen a lot. Two ears and one mouth should tell us something.

In these pages principles, illustrations, and Band-Aids are offered to assist you in the high and holy "calling" of parenting. As we go through this challenging process together, my prayer is that the Holy Spirit will work in your heart and life as He also has worked in mine.

ACKNOWLEDGMENTS

A s with any book there are special people to thank. First and foremost, I want to thank Wallace Henley, who took my sermons and made them sing. His keen insight into popular culture coupled with his biblical wisdom enhanced every chapter.

Thanks also to my assistant, Beverly Gambrell, and secretary, Betty Brockman. Beverly's my "right-hand man" and helps me keep up with my crazy schedule and ever growing deadlines. She helped with proofing and putting the final project together. Betty types my sermons every week. She's the only person who knows what I'm going to say before I say it! These manuscripts form the foundation of my books. My appreciation also goes to Lee Cole, who edited my spoken messages and made them "readable" for this project.

I'm also deeply indebted to the many experts in the field of parenting. I've feasted at the table of these gifted pastors, counselors, authors, and teachers for years and years. Whether from reading, listening, viewing, or conversing, I have gleaned from such greats as James Dobson, Chuck Swindoll, Bill Hybels, Joe Stowell, Jerry Vines, and Adrian Rogers. And what parent cannot learn from his children? Let me thank my boys, Ed, Ben, and Cliff, for being great sons and super sources of real-life illustrations.

Let me add that throughout this book, you will notice that I use the somewhat "politically incorrect" third person *masculine* pronoun when referring to unnamed individuals. Since it's a book about parenting and all my kids are sons, it just comes naturally for me.

Finally, let me thank the folks at Moody Publishers for allowing me this follow-up to my book *The 10 Commandments of Marriage*. I consider it an honor that those at "the name you can trust" put their trust in me once again.

INTRODUCTION

Author and comedienne Gilda Radner told this moving story about a mongrel hound that gave birth to six puppies. The six were all healthy, playful, and happy, but they shared a strange manner of movement.

The pups' walking style had been determined prior to their birth. Seems a human family had adopted the vagrant hound, which soon got pregnant. One day as the dog's new master was mowing his lawn, the pet scampered and played by chasing the lawn mower. On one dash toward the thrashing machine, the dog couldn't stop in time, and her rear legs slid under the mower. The whirring blade whacked them off.

The dog's owner scooped up the hound and her limbs and rushed to the veterinarian. "I can sew her up," said the vet, "or you can put her to sleep if you want. But the puppies are okay. She'll be able to deliver the puppies."[1]

"Do whatever it takes to save her life," said the dog's master.

The veterinarian decided to do even more than that. He reattached the dog's hind legs and sent her home to recover. The old dog was forced to try to learn a new trick: how to walk again. Problem was she couldn't get the hang of the newly sewn rear legs. She would put one front leg forward, then the other, but do nothing with the reattached hind legs. Instead, she'd take two steps, flip up her rump, and move forward.

In a week or so, the puppies were born. The mother hound nursed and weaned them. But when the six dogs learned to walk, they followed the pattern of their mother. The human family would chuckle as they watched the parade of the old dog and her pups: seven dogs with four legs using only the front two and flipping up their rumps behind.

Human parents, too, often pass their dysfunction to their kids—but it's no laughing matter. Life experiences grind and tear; parents get wounded and ripped, and develop negative lifestyles and behavioral patterns. They give birth to children who, though they've not been sucked under the "lawn mower," develop patterns of living as if they had.

David Blankenhorn is talking about "severed" parenting when he discusses, in his book *Fatherless America*, "the dispersal of fatherhood." Blankenhorn notes that some single mothers, in trying to explain to a child why no dad is in the home, convey the idea that a father is merely a sperm donor. Says Blankenhorn:

> First, fatherhood is deconstructed, broken down into its various elements. Over here, making a child. Over there, raising a child. Then the fragments of fatherhood can be spread around to different people.... As a result, the word *father* ceases to be a noun. There is no such thing as a father. Instead, there are people who do fatherlike things.[2]

The result is fractured families suffering limited development, with supportive limbs that ought to be healthy being in a state of atrophy. And many of those families are households with both parents present, but in varying levels of dysfunction. They hobble along through life spiritually, emotionally, mentally, and intellectually. Tragically, their little "pups" stumble along behind them.

It may not be possible to teach old dogs new tricks, but it is possible for parents to overcome the causes of dysfunction and grow into being positive fathers and mothers who pass strength and wholeness to their children.

That's what this book is about. *The 10 Commandments of Parenting,* all based on solid biblical principles, are absolutes. They are not "maybes" but truths rooted in the eternal Word and proven again and again in human experience.

Throughout the book, I recount stories, anecdotes, and illustrations of various parenting experiences. Some are based on direct events and circumstances, while others are compilations of situations with which I or my colleagues have worked. Frequently, I change the names of folks described in the stories, though all the illustrations have found their way into the public domain at some level—either by public testimony or in written form. Illustrations are drawn from actual experiences and are used by direct permission or because they have become a matter of public knowledge, as in a testimony. Where first names only are given, the names are fictitious, though symbolizing actual people or composites.

This book is not just for parents. Young married people anticipating offspring might view the information as "Pre-Parenting 101." Single people will benefit from the principles as they have opportunity to help people with children, or find themselves caring for someone else's kids. The truths penned here will aid teachers challenged with the intellectual nurture of other people's children. Empty nesters will find valuable concepts they can pass to their own children as they become parents. Even teenagers will find principles here that will explain seemingly mysterious parental behaviors and actions.

History bulges with the tragic consequences of poor parenting. More than 12 million people died in World War II, in part, at least, because Adolph Hitler was raised by a cruel father. But human history is also chock-full of the blessings from parents who got it right. Augustine wrote of his mother, Monica, "In the flesh she brought me to birth in this world: in her heart she brought me to birth in (God's) eternal light."[3] There are people, like Winston Churchill, who contributed to history despite poor parenting, but whose children suffered.

On May 16, 2002, President George W. Bush addressed the National Hispanic Prayer Breakfast. He told the group,

> I work the rope lines a lot, and people say, "Mr. President, I pray for you and your family." I turn to them, I look them in the eye, and say, "That's the greatest gift you can give. That's the greatest gift you can give. I mean it with all sincerity."[4]

After someone asked how they could pray for George W. Bush as he carried the crushing burdens of the presidency, he reportedly replied that his basic prayer request was that he would be a godly husband and father.

Nothing could better express the high position of the parenting job and the importance of the absolute principles God has revealed for effective parenting!

A PERSONAL WORD
Thou Shalt Build a Functional Family

This chapter addresses the number one problem in America, which is also the number one problem in the family. It's heavy stuff . . . but it provides the proven formula for building the foundation necessary for a healthy family. Read it carefully and prayerfully.

—E. Y.

Commandment 1

THOU SHALT BUILD A FUNCTIONAL FAMILY

For years I have stated my belief that America's number one problem is the breakdown of the family. Whenever I say that, inevitably some offer a different nomination for America's most pressing dilemma. It doesn't take them long, however, to see that at the foundational root of the problem they name is the family meltdown.

In recent years the plight of our families has been described by a relatively new term: *dysfunctional*. With that in mind, let me state again for the record: I believe America's number one problem is the dysfunctional family. And since society's top problem is dysfunctional families, *our highest priority must be to build functional families.*

Building healthy, functioning families ought to be the consuming passion of any people and their culture—not the national defense or the national economy, not foreign affairs or tax reform. The government can't build functional families. In fact, its policies sometimes stand in the way of developing healthy homes.

People build functional families by following the absolute principles God lays out in His Word. That's why this book is called *The 10 Commandments of Parenting*. We will range the Scripture, exploring God's absolutes for building wholesome, happy, functional families. We'll see that William Bennett is right when he calls the family "the fundamental unit of civilization."[1]

FROM OZZIE AND HARRIET
TO OZZY OSBOURNE

Since the advent of television, there have been widely varying depictions of the family. We've had Ozzie and Harriet, Lucy and Ricky, Beaver Cleaver and his household, Andy, Opie, and Aunt Bee, the Brady Bunch, Sanford and Son, the Huxtables, and many others.

Most of these families focused on functionality and treated today's dysfunctional lifestyles as exceptions. But in recent times, family dysfunction is actually celebrated. The popularity of "The Osbournes" indicates the new twist in pop culture. The hit cable TV program features the family of Ozzy Osbourne, who is described by one writer as "an aging, tattooed, drug-battered monster of rock morph." At one time it was alleged that Ozzy was a devil worshiper.[2] Twelve cameras stationed throughout the Osbourne home catch the daily routine of a family that is anything but routine.

As bizarre as life may seem in Ozzy's household, Los Angeles family therapist Jessica Simmonds found, in some ways, the Osbournes "live a very normal life in this upper-middle-class environment, mixed with a really strange mentality and dysfunction." Simmonds sees a home with a "domineering mother" and a "feeble father." Such are major factors in the equation of dysfunction, and so, says Simmonds, "it's not all funny. . . . There's a lot of sadness here."[3] As there is in dys-functional families everywhere.

DYSFUNCTION IS DANGEROUS

A while back I asked someone what "dysfunctional" meant. "It means nonfunctioning," the person replied. That would seem the obvious meaning, but it's not the precise definition. The prefix *dys* actually means "dangerous." A dysfunctional family, then, by definition, is one functioning "dangerously." Dangerous for whom?

Dangerous for the Children

One study found that children of divorced parents have behavior problems, find it more difficult to adjust, and make lower grades. They also have a higher dropout rate from school and a higher rate of pregnancy out of wedlock.[4]

Columnist Vox Day told of watching MTV videos while working out at his exercise club. There were two different rock bands whose music focused on the impact broken families had on children. Decades ago such songs would not have found such "resonance in the culture," Day wrote. But now, "the terrible costs of divorce linger on, not only in the lives of the divorcing parties but also the lives of the children and the lives of those with whom the children become emotionally involved." Day noted a 1993 study in the *Journal of Family Psychology,* which found a 260 to 340 percent greater likelihood of kids from broken families needing psychological help than those from healthy families.[5]

Dangerous for Husbands and Wives

As family dysfunction has increased, so has domestic violence. Many police officers attend our church. Without exception, the ones I've spoken with will verify that the most frightening, complex, and challenging assignments they have are those involving family fights. Passions run high, fuses are short, and triggers are easily pulled. But it doesn't stop there. Family dysfunction is dangerous for the mental and emotional health of the men and women involved.

Tracy was a beautiful woman in her early forties when she sought help. She was a committed Christian who had been divorced for several years and was raising two children alone. She described her wonderful childhood in a positive, nurturing home. When she grew up she married her "dream husband." But a year into the marriage, her dream husband had become her worst nightmare. He was abusing her physically and emotionally, while having numerous affairs.

She divorced him and later married another man. This one was an alcoholic and drug addict. Desperate to protect her children, she left him. By the time Tracy sought help, the woman who had entered her first marriage with such confidence and joyful anticipation was a trembling human being who doubted her own self-worth and who bore scars in her body evidencing the dangerous places and people with whom she had lived.

Dangerous for Society

Dysfunction is also dangerous for society as a whole. Almost half the people arrested in America in 1999 were under age twenty-five. Between 1965 and 1998, as families imploded, the nation's juvenile crime rate soared at a 175 percent rate.[6] If the family is indeed civilization's fundamental unit, then *each time a family falls into dysfunction there is a threat to a nation's well-being.*

"FORMULA" FOR A FUNCTIONAL FAMILY

In western nations especially, there seems to be a simple formula for building functional families: $N + E + P = FF$. The assumption is that when physical and material *needs (N)* are met from cradle to grave, and people have a good *education (E)* along with ample opportunities for basic *pleasures (P)* such as travel, recreation, and entertainment, the result will be a *functional family (FF)*. But the record of affluent society proves that this formula doesn't compute.

The real equation for a functional family is $C + BP - CU = FF$. That is, *Christ (C)* plus *biblical principles (BP)* minus the *curse (CU)* produces a *functional family (FF)*.

So let's do the "math." In the following chapters we'll go into detail about the importance of Christ and biblical principles in building healthy homes. But first we will look at the beginning in the Garden of Eden—God's perfect plan with the world's first family, Adam and Eve, and the appearance of the deadly problem of . . . *the curse.*

GOD'S PERFECT PLAN

The book of Genesis is foundational. To understand the family, we have to begin with the first family. Prior to their disobedience and the resulting fall of humanity into sin, the Eden family formed a perfect triangle of fellowship among God, Adam, and Eve. Children would have followed naturally in the perfect world because multiplying and scattering were in God's original plan for the beings He had created in His image (see Genesis 1:27–28).

In the Garden of Eden, the first family functioned in four beautiful unities: (1) the unity between God and Adam and Eve, which led to (2) personal unity of each individual with his or her own personality, (3) unity between the two human beings, and (4) unity between people and nature. The unity with God was foundational for all the other unities. The result of all this was positive, wholesome behavior; peace; and joy through God's Spirit.

THE "ALIEN" ENTERS

One day a being alien to this happy family entered Eden. "Do you want to be like God?" the Evil One asked. The two human beings fell for his con. They decided to trade dependence and fellowship with God for the enthronement of self. Adam and Eve moved from dependence on God to self-control and self-rule. The unity with God was broken, evil came in, and the ingredients of dysfunction penetrated the world. *The curse began.*

In 2002, many Americans were stunned when a drifter broke into the blissful home of a Utah family and snatched Ed and Lois Smart's older daughter. For nine months, the family and surrounding community searched for Elizabeth Smart. Finally, and thankfully, she was found and her kidnappers arrested. The vagrant who broke into the Smart home was an alien—a stranger who had no business there.

The suspect had worked one time for the Smart family as a handyman. Later, people were shocked to learn the child had probably been brainwashed to the extent she seemed at times to go along with her kidnappers.

This contemporary episode illustrates what happened in Eden. The Evil One was an intruder in the garden who shattered his way into the hearts of Adam and Eve, stealing them from the One who was the basis for their family relationship, and bringing them into a willful choice of the curse.

FAMILY DYSFUNCTION
FROM BROKEN RELATIONSHIPS

A Broken Relationship with God

The curse continues to impact families today, having many negative effects. First, as fellowship with God is broken, people try to hide from Him. Adam and Eve had once yearned for time with God, just like loving family members who will do almost anything, pay any price, go any distance to be together. But when the curse came, Adam and Eve ran and hid from the One for whose presence they had previously hungered.

Today, we still see human beings trying to hide from God. I've heard all sorts of excuses from people as to why they don't attend church. One man actually told a friend of mine he couldn't join him at church because Sunday was the only day he had to go to his property out in the country and visit his pigs. Now, I've never spent a day visiting pigs. Maybe it's more fun than it sounds. That's only one of the hundreds of excuses I've heard through the years. But actually, the biggest reason people stay away from church is they are just like Adam and Eve—hiding from God. They don't want to know God and they don't want Him to know them. Why? Because they don't want to surrender control of their lives to God.

The foundation of a functional family is a relationship with God, through which He controls the home. When that core relationship is broken, dysfunction can enter.

A Broken Relationship with Ourselves

Another effect of the curse contributing to family dysfunction is the change it brings in our relationship to ourselves. Let's look at a couple of psychological terms. *Psychotics* are people who see others as the problem; *neurotics* are those who see themselves as the problem. Prior to the Fall, Adam and Eve had a healthy self-perception. After the Fall, however, we see Adam as both psychotic and neurotic. His psychosis is revealed in his attempt to blame Eve, and his neurosis is revealed in his personal shame.

So many of our families are made up of people who are either psychotic or neurotic, or both. Now we all know how to play the blame game, which in turn sparks family feuds, fusses, and fights. Or we try to hide by filling our personal lives

25

with all sorts of distractions. But none of this covers the pain and emptiness we feel inside. We realize we are living in rebellion against God, and that brings shame and feelings of guilt.

Take the case of Carrie. She and her husband, Jack, a wealthy business owner, had a rebellious son. One day Carrie began to understand how some of her own ungodly behaviors and attitudes were being imitated by her son. (Sometimes, guilt is real and not a neurotic fantasy.) But rather than dealing with her sin and her son, Carrie ran—not in a literal sense but certainly in a practical one. She gave all her time and energy to becoming her community's greatest teacher of arts and crafts. She conducted seminars and enjoyed the acclaim of women who sat at her feet and learned the hobby she had mastered. She was never home, so her relationship with her son and husband began to crumble. But Carrie wasn't running from her husband and son. Because of the shame she felt, she was running from God . . . until one horrible day when Carrie came home to find her son had committed suicide.

A Broken Relationship with Others

A third effect of the curse on families today is the breaking of our relationships with others. Initially, Adam and Eve enjoyed a harmonious relationship. But after the Fall, the first thing we see is the psychotic behavior of blame. When God confronted Adam, he blamed Eve. When God turned to Eve, she blamed the serpent. And both of them had the audacity to try to blame God.

Much of the dysfunction in Jack and Carrie's home was in blaming one another for their son's behavior. Later, it became evident he killed himself partly because he blamed himself for the inability of his mother and father to get along. Yes, the curse disrupts our relationship with others.

A GALAXY OF DYSFUNCTION

None of this is new. Survey the constellation of Old Testament patriarchs, from Abraham to Jacob, and you find an array of dysfunctional families. The patriarchs and their progeny show that the curse expresses itself in different ways in different families, and is passed on from generation to generation. In some families, the curse showed up as physical abuse; in others, emotional torment; in yet others, alcoholism and drug addiction. The curse recycled in the children until one generation finally rose up and cried, "Enough!" That generation repented and turned to God, and the curse was broken from the family line, unless a subsequent generation rebelled against the Lord.

Dysfunction Intensifies

This is the point of what God showed Moses in Exodus 34. God spoke to Moses in a vision: "The Lord, the Lord God, compassionate and gracious, slow to anger, and abounding in lovingkindness and truth" (verse 6). It was sweet music on Moses' ears to know the core nature of God is compassion, grace, slowness to get angry, and overflowing love and kindness. Who wouldn't want a God like that?

In the vision, God continued by revealing He "keeps lovingkindness for thousands, . . . forgives iniquity, transgression and sin" (verse 7). So far, everyone would applaud this gracious God who allows people to do their "own thing." But then comes another insight into God's ways. God tells Moses that despite His loving-kindness and graciousness, "He will by no means leave the guilty unpunished, visiting the iniquity of fathers on the children and on the grandchildren to the third and fourth generations" (verse 7).

Humans, with their God-given freedom, choose the curse, and God, who honors human freedom, allows it to go forward, though He constantly warns of its effects and calls people to repentance. This mounting pile of consequences from the curse means family dysfunction intensifies. The hurting people wonder if the curse can be broken and the cycle halted.

Canceling the Curse

Clearly, the first element in building a functional family is to cancel the curse. When we indicate Christ plus biblical principles minus the curse equals a functional family *(C + BP - CU = FF)*, we're suggesting the impact of the curse can be canceled. We do this by (1) confessing our personal and family sins, (2) turning away from the sin that is the effect of the curse, and (3) turning to God through Christ. Because God *is* full of loving-kindness and graciousness, He receives and forgives us even when we are crying out because we are face-to-face with the disastrous consequences of our dysfunction.

Perhaps as you read these words you are realizing you need to declare, "The cycle ends right here!"

Eventually Jacob did just that. One of the "stars" in the patriarchal constellation, Jacob had three great encounters with God. The first was at Bethel, which means "house of God." Ironically, he was there under a ruse. Jacob had left his parents ostensibly to find a wife, but actually he was running away from his brother, Esau, whom he had tricked. Night fell, and young Jacob was far from home and scared. In his desperation, he prayed. As he did, a vision unfolded, and he saw a stairway to heaven, with angels going up and down, symbolizing Jacob's prayers going up and God's response coming down. Though Jacob had been a con artist and scoundrel all his life, God said:

> "Your descendants will also be like the dust of the earth, and you will spread out to the west and to the east and to the north and to the south; and in you and in your descendants shall all the families of the earth be blessed. Behold, I am with you, and

will keep you wherever you go, and will bring you back to this land; for I will not leave you until I have done what I have promised you." (Genesis 28:14–15)

When Blessing and Curse Collide

The blessing of God is the precise opposite, the antithesis, of the curse from the devil. Scientists tell us that when matter and antimatter collide, cataclysmic destruction occurs. When the blessing of God smacks into the curse of the Evil One, the curse is destroyed!

But Jacob didn't deserve God's blessing—and neither do we. However, God is gracious and merciful, and when we return to Him, even with impure motives, He will hear us and break the curse of dysfunction from our families. Now, rather than mounting curses, we enter the buildup of blessing.

Jacob's second great experience with God was near a place he named Mahanaim. As he neared the Jordan River, Jacob remembered Esau had vowed to kill him, so he decided to check his brother's mood before he took another step. He sent scouts ahead, and after what must have been a nail-biting time for Jacob, they returned with a chilling message: "Esau is coming after you with four hundred thugs!" (Genesis 32:6, paraphrase).

Jacob was terrified. Again he sought God in prayer, asking for favor with his brother. But Jacob, wheeler and dealer that he was, decided to hedge his bet and buy off his brother. So he sent lavish gifts ahead to Esau. In the meantime, he plotted a survival strategy in case prayer and bribery didn't work. He divided his family and flocks into two separate groups, figuring if Esau attacked the first group, the second would get away, and Jacob would at least have something left. He sent everyone across the River Jabbok, but he stayed behind.

Now Jacob was alone again, as he was that night twenty years earlier at Bethel. His back was against the wall. He couldn't go backward or forward, so he went to his knees. Like many people suddenly in a dark alley alone with the monstrous consequences of their dysfunction, Jacob learned to pray on the fast track. Often people scoff at this kind of desperate, "foxhole" praying. God doesn't. He knows "our frame" and that we are "dust," understanding better than we our limitations and shortcomings (Psalm 103:14). If God didn't hear prayers of desperation, not many of us would be saved.

A Supernatural "Smackdown"

While Jacob prayed, he experienced what theologians call a "theophany," or an appearance of God in some particular form, such as an angel. Suddenly Jacob felt a rugged, muscular hand on his shoulder. The ground became an arena for a supernatural "smackdown" as this being wrestled Jacob to the ground. The prize from this bout would be nothing less than control of Jacob's life. God wrestled Jacob because God wanted Jacob to give his life completely over to His control. This was round 2—or 2,000 or 2 million—of the same match that began in the garden when Adam and Eve found themselves a tag team going up against God. Smooth, suave, debonair Jacob had skated through life on the wheels of his own skill, craftiness, intellect, charm, and chicanery, doing his own thing, controlling his own destiny. But that brought only dysfunction to his life and everything he touched. Now he is on the ground, struggling with who knows what.

The angel squeezes Jacob, and out come the components of dysfunction—ego, pride, self-sufficiency, vanity, falseness, hypocrisy, and greed. Yet Jacob doesn't want to give in. He wants to retain control. Finally, Jacob feels a sharp pain in his thigh as his opponent dislocates his hip.

As dawn breaks, Jacob's Wrestler knows it's time to relent, but Jacob is hanging on with clawing persistence. Jacob agrees to let his opponent go if the supernatural Wrestler will bless him. "Your name shall no longer be Jacob [Cheater]," says the powerful Being, "but Israel [one who strives with God]" (Genesis 32:26–28). Jacob is left with lameness so he will always remember his dependence on God. Now, with the Lord's help, Jacob is ready to end the cycle of his dysfunction.

The next day, Jacob sees Esau closing in with his four hundred men. Jacob—Israel—musters all the courage he can and limps out to meet Esau.

Esau runs toward Jacob, embraces him with a kiss, and they both weep (Genesis 33:4). Because Jacob surrenders control to God, God brings healing in the broken relationship.

IMPORTANT LESSONS

There are many important lessons here for building functional families. Years earlier, at Bethel, Jacob had made an initial decision to give God control, but he had not followed through. For many of us, there is a point of beginning with God, but we fail to walk in the reality of our commitment, and the old ways return. Jesus said a person who had been freed of a demon but puts nothing in the place the demon had occupied and controlled, would find himself later in a worse state than the original (Matthew 12:43–45). So a profound lesson for families seeking to be healed of dysfunction is the importance of *putting into practice* the advantages of a relationship with God.

Accepting Our Weakness

In building functional families, one of the greatest things we can do is revel in our lameness! The devil will always try to convince us we are not capable of raising healthy families, that we are too sinful, inadequate, and stupid. Popular culture will sing Satan's song to us, telling us we need experts, a "village," or some other add-on to build a functional family. Jesus says we are to agree with our "adversary quickly" (Matthew 5:25 KJV). So we should acknowledge that we, alone, are not up to the job of building functional families. But our "lameness" —our weakness—is actually our strength, for then we depend on God for every step.

Remember, God has said that if we would acknowledge Him in all our ways, and lean on Him rather than our own understanding, He would direct our paths (Proverbs 3:5–6). That means, as we'll see in this book, following His revealed principles to build strong, healthy households.

Seeing Our Struggles as Opportunities

Another important lesson about building functional families is that we must begin to see struggles as opportunities for blessing. God loves us enough to "wrestle" with us. Those He loves, He disciplines (Hebrews 12:6). To Jacob's credit, rather than crying out against his opponent or being bitter about his struggle, he asks the divine Wrestler to bless him. God's way in the life of those who turn to Him is to use adversity to strengthen and bless. Jacob gets the point, and so must we if we are going to build functional families.

FROM DYSFUNCTION
TO HEALTHY FUNCTIONALITY

The healing of Jacob's relationship with his brother, Esau, had an impact on his children and reveals the shift from dysfunction to healthy functionality in their family. This brings us to Jacob's third great experience with God. This one took place in Egypt when he was an old man.

Jacob had a tent full of sons. One of these sons, Joseph, was his favorite—and it showed. Now you would think Jacob would have known better since it was his father's favoritism that played such a big role in his own painful relationship with his brother, Esau. Nonetheless, Jacob continued to heap parental accolades and approval onto Joseph.

Joseph's gloating attitude did not help matters either. He had special dreams that he bragged about to his brothers—one of which had his brothers bowing to him as their ruler! During this period of family dysfunction in Jacob's household, the jealousy and resentment of his sons toward the favored Joseph grew daily.

Finally, the sibling rivalry reached a boiling point, and Jacob's sons plotted to get rid of their bratty, arrogant little brother. So they sold Joseph into slavery to a caravan of Ismaelites and told Jacob that a wild beast had devoured his beloved son.

Joseph's relationship with God became stronger during his slavery. It was this strong relationship that would not only bring healing to his broken family but also save them from starvation.

Joseph's story in Egypt started off great. Sold to a nobleman named Potiphar, who was captain of Pharaoh's guard, Joseph quickly found favor with Potiphar and was put in charge of the entire household.

Unfortunately, Potiphar's wife was an immoral woman who falsely accused Joseph of rape. So he was imprisoned for a crime he did not commit. After at least two years of prison, Joseph was released through supernatural intervention. Pharaoh had asked Joseph to interpret a disturbing dream he was having. With God's help, Joseph was able to do it, and Pharaoh was so pleased he promoted Joseph to prime minister, the second most powerful position in Egypt.

Meanwhile, back home in Canaan, a terrible famine swept the land. So Jacob sent his sons down to Egypt where he had heard there was sufficient food. When they arrived, Jacob's sons had to plead for food before—you guessed it—the prime minister! Many years had passed, so they did not recognize their long-lost brother.

Now if I'm Joseph, I'm thinking, "It's payback time!" But not Joseph; he refused to take on the victim role and instead assumed the task of healer.

Joseph took responsibility for his own life and knew his brothers must take the same responsibility for theirs. So he decided to take action to bring them to repentance. The struggles he had experienced in Egypt were the very dynamics that had established him in a deep relationship with God. Joseph didn't want his brothers to have to go to the depths to which he himself had plunged, but he did want them to have opportunity to know God as he did.

So Joseph first falsely accused his brothers of stealing, as he had been accused falsely. Second, he had them thrown in jail, as he had been. Finally, he sent all his brothers back to Canaan, except for Simeon, knowing this would guarantee their return. Joseph told them to bring Benjamin, the youngest brother, when they came back to Egypt (see Genesis 42:8–26).

On their return home, Joseph's brothers told their father, Jacob, all that had happened. Reluctantly, Jacob allowed his sons to return to Egypt with Benjamin. Once there, Joseph revealed his true identity to his brothers. Immediately, there was repentance and healing in that dysfunctional family (see Genesis 42:27–45:15). Joseph became the person in his generation who broke the curse-cycle from his family.

A VITAL PRINCIPLE

Some may judge Joseph harshly for his treatment of his brothers. But Joseph's own suffering had shown him a vital principle at the heart of healing dysfunction: If the curse is to be healed, there must be confession and genuine repentance before there can be forgiveness and restoration.

This is one of the hardest lessons in moving family members from dysfunction to function. *Sometimes people have to be allowed to experience the full brunt of their dysfunctional behavior before there's any hope of healing.* Joseph knew this and was patient enough not to rush the process.

After the reunion in Egypt, Joseph sent his brothers home to Canaan to get Jacob and the whole family. When the brothers reported to Jacob, they confessed they had sold Joseph into slavery. Jacob had long grieved for his son, and now his sorrow could heal. The brothers too, forgiven, restored, and rid of the guilt they had carried for years, could enter the healing process. Jacob and his kids started looking like a family again.

THE GREAT HEALER

Joseph points us to the great Healer, Jesus Christ. As Joseph was the key to breaking the curse of dysfunction in his family, Jesus Christ has the power to shatter the curse in every person who comes to Him. This is because Jesus, on the cross, became the very embodiment of the curse on each of us from the very time of Adam (Galatians 3:13). For every person who freely and willingly receives Christ, the curse is displaced by the blessing of God. But to get the benefit of this removal of the curse, we must remember the mistake of Jacob. At Bethel, he received God's blessing, but didn't act upon it until twenty years later, when he yielded himself afresh to God at Mahanaim. So, having received Christ and the blessing of God that displaces the curse, we must behave in a way that is consistent with our identity in Christ if we are to enjoy the fruit of functionality.

Jacob became "Limping Israel," beginning a process that enabled his son Joseph to *run*. The curse was broken. When we say "enough" to dysfunction, we—and our entire family—can understand the words of the great old hymn: "He breaks the power of canceled sin, He sets the prisoner free."[7]

QUESTIONS FOR PARENTS

1. What are symptoms of dysfunction in your family you need to deal with as a parent?

2. Apply the "formula"—*C (Christ) + BP (Biblical Principles) – CU (The Curse) = FF (Functional Family)*—to your family life, and answer these questions:

   - Have we as parents committed ourselves and our home to Christ?

   - Are we as parents growing in our understanding and application of biblical principles in parenting?

   - Are we as parents identifying and repenting of the effects of the curse in our own lives?

A PERSONAL WORD
Thou Shalt Love Thy Children

Most parents think this commandment is a given. Everyone loves their children, right? It's more than just saying the words and meeting their needs, however. It's about sowing seeds that will bear fruit in their lives. Our families are gardens. We need to evaluate the quality and quantity of love we've sown into our children.

—E. Y.

Commandment 2

THOU SHALT LOVE THY CHILDREN

A t retirement parties, people give testimonials to departing long-time employees. Sometimes a retiree's associates are glad to see him go and don't have much to say. At other retirement farewells, there are tears and toasts and tales of triumph. Retirement parties are good opportunities for people to know how their close associates view them.

There are no retirement festivities or farewell banquets for parents. Take it from me, the job is never done. When our children are young, parenting is of the direct, in-your-face (yours and theirs) variety. When our offspring are grown, they're still our kids, and, though the weight of child-rearing might be lighter, we remain parents as long as blood flows in our veins.

Now imagine for a moment there *is* such a thing as parental retirement parties and that one is being held just for you. You enter the banquet room and there they all are—your kids—all grown up and ready to share their testimonials.

PARENTAL "RETIREMENT PARTY"

You smile and tense up a bit. Actually, I'm breaking out into a sweat as I imagine myself in this situation! You don't know if you're about to be roasted or toasted!

Consider this for a moment: *If your children were giving you a retirement-from-parenting party, what would they say about you in their testimonials?*

Whew! That's a sobering thought. Would you and I hear tributes or rebukes? Our children's testimonies about us would be a barometer of the relationship we had with them in their growing-up years. Their comments would reflect their perception of the love they received from us. By the way, if you're just beginning your journey as a parent, consider yourself blessed! You have the opportunity, right from the start, to put into practice our next commandment of parenting: *Thou shalt love thy children.*

RE-SOWING WITH THE SEED OF LOVE

Love is the greatest blessing enjoyed by people liberated from the curse of the Fall. And the family is the garden where love grows and bears its fruit. It's important, then, for us to evaluate the quality and quantity of love we've sown into our children.

Some of you reading this book know the importance and immense challenge of trying to re-sow the ground with love and recover relationships after the children are grown. That's important, too. In fact, wherever you might be in the parenting process, it's vital to plant huge crops of love seed.

Many parents conclude this principle of loving their children is a "no-brainer." They might say something like, "Loving my children is the easiest thing in the world to do! I meet their needs, sprinkle in a little discipline here and there, occasionally satisfy a few of their wants, and that's all there is

to it." But many parents who have followed that very proce-
dure discover their kids don't have a clue about love.

Angela had raised her daughter Lisa Ann with all the frills
a little girl loves. She saw to it that she learned everything from
ballet to baton twirling to baking. So she was shocked one day
to learn that her now grown daughter was seeing a professional counselor to discuss her "unhappy childhood."

"I never felt loved," said Lisa Ann, when she finally confronted her mother.

"How could that be?" gasped a shocked Angela. "I gave you
everything!"

"But it was all about *you!*" Lisa Ann shot back. "*You* chose
all those fancy clothes for me and made me take ballet. You
never asked me what I wanted to do. I wanted to wear blue
jeans and play basketball!"

Angela was shocked at her daughter's bitterness, but she
faced the hard truth that she had failed to convey to Lisa Ann
how much she loved her.

FRESH INSIGHTS FROM ANCIENT PARENTS

An ancient set of parents—Abraham and Sarah—teach us
a lot about loving kids in the way they related to their son,
Isaac. They show that parental love may be different from
what we expect.

Waiting to Become Parents

At age seventy-five, Abraham had no children (Genesis
12:4; the story of Abraham's promised and delivered son is told
in Genesis 12–21). Then God promised him he would have a
special son. Ten years passed, and he still had no offspring.[1]
But God was still promising, and at age ninety-nine there was
God again, with the promise of that son. By then Abraham had
every reason to believe his gene-pool was as dry as the desert
in which he lived, but the Lord reaffirmed His promise by

41

actually changing the old man's name from "Abram" ("esteemed father") to "Abraham" ("father of multitudes").

Overhearing this promise, Abraham's wife, Sarah, laughed to herself. After all, she was ninety! However, God reassured both Abraham and Sarah that they would have a son (Genesis 18:10–14).

Just when things looked impossible, God stepped in. Sarah got pregnant! One year after God promised a child, Sarah gave birth to a son. When the child was born, Abraham and Sarah named him "Isaac," meaning "laughter." That's because when the Lord told ninety-year-old Sarah she would have a child, she laughed.

Now we begin to see the ways by which this old but freshly energized couple showed love for their child.

Provide Your Children Identity

First, they had Isaac circumcised (Genesis 21:4). Having an infant cut at a sensitive place might not seem very loving. Actually, this was a huge demonstration of love by Abraham and Sarah for Isaac. *By this act, they gave their son an identity.* Circumcision was the way Abraham and his descendants would mark themselves as being in a special covenant relationship with God (Genesis 17:10). It showed that Abraham and his family were set apart for God's special purpose, with a unique role in God's plan for bringing redemption to humanity—even though Abraham didn't understand it all. So, by having Isaac circumcised, Abraham was saying, "Isaac, you have an identity. You are part of a special family—the family of God!"

Humans long to discover who they are and where they belong. Many spend their entire lives trying to "find themselves"—searching for an identity. Those who don't have a strong sense of identity get confused about who they really are. Often they adopt one identity, then another, bobbing through life from one self-concept to another, tormented by the inconsistency (and often tormenting those dearest to them).

Identity confusion is starkly evident in this generation in the changing concepts of masculinity and femininity. Family advocate and author James Dobson notes that the awkwardness being felt with the revision of relationships between sexes is not a trivial matter but goes straight to our identity and self-awareness. Dobson writes that these concepts have long-term implications.

> Human beings are sexual creatures, both physically and psychologically. Our very identity ("Who am I?") begins with gender assignment and the understanding of what it means to be masculine or feminine. Virtually every aspect of life is related to this biological foundation. . . . Any revolution of such proportions is certain to have far-reaching consequences for the family and the culture in which it exists. How can we expect to preserve social order when the rules governing our sexual behavior are turned upside down?[2]

To love our children, then, is to establish them in a strong identity so they can live with stability and confidence in an identity-assaulting, confusing world. If our kids have a strong sense of who they are, they will not allow others to categorize or define their personalities, or force them into a warped mold.

DEVELOPING YOUR CHILDREN'S IDENTITY

1. Understand How Your Children Feel

To establish your children in a strong, positive identity, first *you must understand how they feel*. Whenever a child says to a parent, "You just don't understand," warning bells ought to go off in that parent's mind. This is not to say our children are always right about what they feel. However, the basic step to helping a person is to deal with his or her perceptions. The child who says his parent doesn't understand may be crying out to be listened to—and heard. Whenever our kids say that to us, most of us do the easiest thing—get angry and walk away. After all, it's always easier to react than to understand. Let me suggest a better response:

Child: "You just don't understand me!"
Parent: "What is it you think I don't understand?"
Child: "The way I feel."
Parent: "OK. Then let's go somewhere where we can be alone and I can concentrate totally on what you're trying to tell me."

James gives this counsel: "But everyone must be quick to hear, slow to speak and slow to anger" (1:19). I think that is especially true for parents. Children will break your rules and your heart, but when you link with their feelings, a connection is established that makes healing a lot easier.

Jesus Christ, during His ministry in this world, displayed a magnetic personality. He related to people's feelings. When they cried, He cried; when they celebrated, Jesus celebrated with them (John 11:32–36; 2:1–11). This doesn't mean He was controlled by people's feelings but that He understood them and identified with them. As parents, we should not be slaves to our children's feelings, but at the same time we should not send out signals of insensitivity. Neither should we fall into patterns of leniency but of listening. We first need to listen to our kids and get in touch with their feelings before we rush in to fix everything or to discipline.

In doing so, our children develop the identity of being important and significant. Unconsciously, they realize they are important enough for a father or mother to listen to them, and that their feelings are of such significance that their parents are willing to set aside time and effort to understand them. The indulgent parent will produce a child with an identity of self-centeredness, while a listening and understanding father or mother will raise a child with an identity of healthy self-respect.

2. Make Your Children Feel Secure

The second thing you can do to give your kids a healthy, positive identity is *to help them feel secure.* Unconditional love is the primary means of helping any child feel safe and protected.

Some of the saddest results of seventy-five years of communism appeared in the orphanages of Eastern Europe, full of frightened, cowering children. Atheism and the idea of a collective society, which deprived parents of their unique roles in bringing up their children and encouraged family members to spy on one another, robbed families of their warmth. The devaluing of human beings to mere cogs in the revolutionary machine meant that children could be cast aside. When humanitarian agencies began to move into the orphanages after the fall of communism, they found children who were underdeveloped and grimly silent. These precious young ones were afraid of everything because they had never been loved unconditionally.

The surest way to produce a child with an identity of fear and insecurity is to imply there's an "if" attached to our love. A friend of mine had a seventeen-year-old son who became a weight lifter. He couldn't discipline his son physically because the boy was much stronger than he was. He tried grounding him, taking away privileges, lecturing him—nothing seemed to work. Finally, he took him to lunch one day and pulled out a sheet of paper.

"One of the best ways I can help you now," he said, "is to

prepare you for the business world, where you will work. From now on, your life will revolve around this job description. If you learn to follow it, you will succeed in the jobs you will hold someday."

The paper was labeled *"Job Title: Son."* The teen read the document, which stipulated the chores, tasks, expectations, and responsibilities he would have—such as taking out garbage and observing curfews set by the father. The boy read down to the section where his father had written this conclusion:

> Nothing in this document relates to whether I will love you or not. Whether or not you fulfill all the expectations and requirements of this job description, I will love you the same. You can never be fired from this job; you will always be my beloved son.

That young man grew up with a strong, confident identity and became a top executive in a global corporation. In fact, he was promoted on an accelerated basis as his superiors observed his ability to lead others. Because he knew unconditional love from his dad, he felt safe and nonthreatened and therefore could relate positively to other people.

My own mother had four sisters. When I was growing up, I watched them compete with one another. It seemed they were always trying to play the game of one-upmanship. But Aunt Gladys was different. Somehow, she stayed above the silly frays. It was because she loved all her sisters unconditionally—a love she had learned at the feet of Jesus Christ. Aunt Gladys glowed inwardly from her own overwhelming sense of God's grace in her personal life. She had spent many years away from God, and when she returned to Him, she found herself in an unfathomable ocean of grace. In turn, that gave her a love for everyone. When I was around Aunt Gladys, I always felt secure because I knew she loved me unconditionally.

We should give our children heaps of grace. That's the way Jesus Christ loves us. When we become childish and stray from His will, He does not use shame and the threat of rejection to discipline us. He listens to us and touches us with grace—acts of unexpected love that we don't deserve. He encountered a promiscuous Samaritan woman at a well. Rather than blasting her for the sin He knew she had committed, Jesus talked with her, listening carefully and responding truthfully but gently until she turned her life in a new direction (see John 4:1–26). Another woman was brought to Him after she had been caught in a humiliating, sinful moment. Jesus stooped down to where she lay in the dust, had a few words for her, and encouraged her to go her way and sin no more (see John 8:1–11).

True, the Lord, through the Holy Spirit, will discipline us when we sin. But it is always a dimension of His love. In fact, discipline is essential for helping a child feel secure. A youngster with no boundaries cannot feel safe, because not only do boundaries set limits for the child, they also provide protective barriers against those who would bring harm. This is why love and discipline are linked. The writer of Hebrews says those whom God loves He disciplines (Hebrews 12:6). Love-based discipline is corrective, rather than merely punitive. It says to a child, "You are worth correcting." That conveys a secure sense of identity and significance.

3. Make Your Children Feel Significant

In fact, *making a child feel significant* is the third means of establishing a positive sense of identity in a youngster. We do this through praise. Putting their crayon drawings on the family refrigerator is an indirect way of conveying positive thoughts to our children. But we need to open our mouths and speak our affirmations as well. Every child should hear from his or her parent the words "Good job!"

Ronnie and Eddie were ten-year-olds who played on the same basketball team. Ronnie was aggressive and fast, while Eddie was more of a "plodder" who calculated every move before he acted.

When Ronnie missed a basket, he could hear his dad's voice booming from the stands, "How could you miss that shot? Are you blind? Have you forgotten everything I taught you?"

Eddie rarely got the ball, but because of his size and determined, slow movements, he actually developed into an asset for his team's zone defense. He would stand in the area of the basket with his arms in the air blocking the lane and the other team's players who would thud into the wall of his set body. He missed most of the shots he tried, but his father never humiliated him. Instead, Eddie's dad would cheer every strong defensive play his son made and work with Eddie to improve his offensive skills. Rather than harping on what his son could not do, he chose to praise what Eddie did well and help him sharpen the skills he lacked.

Ronnie often left games in tears, grimacing at the thought of missed baskets and lost opportunities. Eddie almost always departed the gym happy and ready to take on the next challenge. He knew he was not the team's top scorer, but it didn't matter. Eddie knew he played a significant role because he had an identity strong in the sense of significance. As far as he was concerned, his team couldn't get along without him!

Catch your children doing something right! Balance positive correction and discipline with heaps of praise. Children who never hear affirmation from their parents react in one of two ways (and sometimes both): They rebel, or they have such a low opinion of themselves they expect to fail at all they do.

LESSONS FROM MOUNT MORIAH

Isaac's parents didn't "program" him for failure. Not only did they love him enough to establish in him a positive and strong self-identity, but *they set the example for their boy in their own lifestyle.*

Model Faith for Your Children

The final two lessons on parenting we can learn from Abraham come from his journey with Isaac up a mountainside. Abraham may have been too old to play ball with Isaac, but he loved that boy with all the enthusiasm of a dad who had waited ninety-nine years to have a son. Yet the day came when Abraham heard God commanding him to take his boy up on a peak called Mount Moriah and sacrifice him! (The story is recorded in Genesis 22.)

Imagine the struggle in Abraham's mind. *Was that really God's voice?* Isaac was supposed to be the child of promise, the first of all those descendants who pile up on the beach of history like sand on a seashore. *What sense would it make to kill my son before he's grown?* The big quandary before Abraham was this: *Do I obey God and lose my son, or disobey God?*

One of the advantages of growing older is that we can look back down the life road we've traveled and recall significant events, lessons learned, and transforming encounters. Abraham could look back in time and see again and again God's faithfulness. What did he see? God's sovereignty. God had been there when He struck a covenant with Abraham. He had been there when Abraham and Sarah went down to Egypt. Wherever they had gone, God had been their world, and they were never without Him and His guidance. Abraham decided to act in accordance with his heroic faith; he would obey God.

So Abraham loaded his donkey, bundled up Isaac, and off they went to Mount Moriah. At its base, Abraham told the servants to wait as he and Isaac began the climb up the rugged hill.

Apparently Isaac was taking inventory and noted that his dad had all the items for a sacrifice except one—the sacrificial lamb. "We have the wood and the fire, but where's the lamb?" the young man asked.

"God will provide," answered Abraham.

At the crest of Moriah, Abraham built an altar, laid the wood on the fire, and tied up Isaac. Earlier, we pondered what Abraham might have been thinking, but what was going on in Isaac's mind? He was a teenager, or perhaps even a young adult by then, and easily could have resisted a man well over one hundred, as Abraham would have been at that point. But there's no record that Isaac fought back. Surely the calculations had added up in his mind: *An altar, firewood. I'm bound up; there's no sacrificial lamb. . . . That must mean I am the sacrifice.*

Now Abraham gets under his tied-up son, lifts and heaves him over onto the altar. Can you imagine the look on Isaac's face when his father lifts the knife above his body?

But just as Abraham tenses his muscles to drive the dagger into Isaac's heart, God speaks: "Do not stretch out your hand against the lad, and do nothing to him; for now I know that you fear God, since you have not withheld your son, your only son, from Me" (Genesis 22:12). Abraham and Isaac hardly have time to let out gigantic sighs of relief when they hear a ram struggling in a thicket. Abraham looses Isaac and sacrifices the ram in his place.

I don't think Isaac ever forgot that experience. When he died at age 180, I believe he could still smell the burning ram. Isaac learned a lesson that day on Moriah that transformed his life. He saw clearly that God had first place, top priority in the lives of his mom and dad. Abraham and Sarah modeled faith for their son.

It takes a "Moriah experience" to accomplish that—those moments in our lives when things seem impossible. In these moments, our kids have occasion to see the extent to which we obey and trust God. It gives us an opportunity to model faith.

Build Your Altars

Abraham was the progenitor of faith and the picture of faithful obedience. One biblical phrase captures the secret of his success: Abraham "pitched his tent . . . and there he built an altar to the Lord" (Genesis 12:8). It is through this practice that Abraham shows us a third way to love our children. *Loving parents leave a legacy for their kids.*

Abraham understood that this world was not his home. He was just passing through, "for he was looking for the city which has foundations, whose architect and builder is God" (Hebrews 11:10). He knew he would find no such city in this world, so he never called a real estate agent, never built a home—he simply pitched a tent. He refused to become attached to the things of this world. Instead, Abraham's focus was on God's will for his life. He wanted his children and grandchildren to know that it is the things of God that are permanent—not the things of this world. That's why, wherever he went, Abraham did not merely pitch his tent, but he also *built* his altar.

The problem is, far too many of us do the exact opposite of Abraham—we *build our tents* and *pitch our altars.* We attach permanence to our homes, our lands, our possessions, and our culture while treating the things of God as ethereal and unreal. We spend our time building, improving, and adding to our tents, and, at best, we "pitch our altars" if we do anything with them at all. Too many of us tend to follow the example of Lot more than Abraham.

Abraham's nephew, Lot, was with him almost as much as a natural-born son. Both were herdsmen, so between them they had a huge number of animals. Their wranglers kept crossing up one another, so Abraham knew that something was going to have to give. The land simply would not sustain the concentration of their herds. So Abraham approached Lot. "Look," he said, "to avoid any conflict, you go one way, and I'll go the other. It doesn't matter which way you choose, just let me know so I'll know where to take my herds and workers" (Genesis 13:8–9, author paraphrase).

The Bible says that Lot *looked toward* Sodom in the Jordan valley, with its lush land and promise of prosperity. This left Uncle Abraham with the craggy, dry barrenness toward the mountains. So Lot separated from Abraham, took his herds down by the Jordan, and settled in the cities of the plain. The Bible says there Lot "pitched his tent toward Sodom" (Genesis 13:12 KJV). The next time we see Lot, he's no longer in a tent pitched outside Sodom—he and his family are in a house, *built in* Sodom.

Lot had moved his family into the city that was considered the red-light district of the whole region. Tragically, something else happened—Sodom moved into Lot and his family. Seems it works that way all the time . . . even today. It starts with a look toward Sodom with all of its possibilities, prosperity, and perversions. Then we "pitch our tents toward Sodom." Nothing permanent—we just want to be close enough to capitalize on the "opportunities" offered there. Better chances to make bigger piles of money or have more "fun." Until we become overconfident and move into Sodom, believing somehow we are impervious to the moral decay surrounding us. But eventually it seeps in, and we wake up one day to discover that Sodom has moved into us.

Later in Genesis we see the disastrous outcome of Lot's family. When he receives the news of God's judgment and impending destruction of the city, Lot has a hard time convincing his family to flee Sodom. He had lost his spiritual credibility with his family. Remember, unlike Abraham, Lot had built his tent . . . and only pitched his altar. Lot's choices resulted in a sorry legacy for his family. And it all started with just a look toward Sodom.

Many parents get so embedded in the world that when God calls them to let go and move their family on to a better place, they find it impossible to uproot. Like Lot, Sodom has seeped into their hearts and minds. Abraham, the father of faith, saw himself as a sturdy ship on which his family sailed through the sea of time and space, and God as the wind. Following God was his highest aim, and that's the legacy Abraham left his family.

NO GREATER LEGACY

Jerry Clower, the late comedian from Yazoo City, Mississippi, used to say, "Every son and daughter ought to be able to stand up flatfooted and say, 'My pappy was a godly man.'" I like that! There is no greater legacy a father and mother can leave behind than to have lived before their children as godly people.

History proves it. Some years ago a team of New York sociologists performed a study of two families, beginning in the eighteenth century and coming all the way into the twentieth century. They wanted to see if a legacy—positive or negative —could indeed be passed from generation to generation. So the researchers traced descendants of the two families over the two-hundred-year period.

Max Jukes was an atheist and his wife an agnostic. The researchers studied 1,200 descendants of this tough-minded, mean-spirited couple. Here is a sampling of the Jukes legacy:

- Of the 1,200, 440 descendants lived in outright debauchery.
- 310 were paupers or vagrants.

- 190 were prostitutes.
- 130 were convicted as criminals.
- 100 were alcoholics.
- More than 100 were habitual thieves.
- 55 suffered sexually transmitted diseases.
- Seven were murderers.

A contemporary of Max Jukes was Jonathan Edwards, pastor, missionary, president of Princeton University, and perhaps the most brilliant theologian in America's history. Edwards and his wife, Sarah, passed a godly legacy to their descendants. As the researchers scanned the generations descending from Jonathan and Sarah Edwards, here is what they found:

- More than 300 were pastors, missionaries, or theologians.
- More than 120 were professors.
- Some 110 were lawyers.
- There were 60 physicians.
- Another 60 were authors of positive, helpful books.
- 30 were judges.
- 14 were university presidents.
- Many were giants of industry.
- Three were members of Congress.
- One was vice president of the United States.[3]

The simple fact is the people in the Jonathan Edwards line had happier, more prosperous and peaceful lives than those in the Jukes line. Parents who really love their children always look far down time's road and consider what life should be like for their offspring.

Out of that love, such parents prepare their children with a positive identity, teach them through a clear example, and leave them with a rich legacy—a legacy of a mom and dad who "pitch their tents" and "build their altars."

These are the parents who will make a difference in time and eternity. These are the parents who really love their children!

QUESTIONS FOR PARENTS

1. If your kids gave you a "parenting retirement party," what are some of the tributes they would give you? (In other words, what would they say you got right in parenting?)

2. In your "retirement speech," what would you point to from your experience of raising your children that showed them how much you loved them back then?

3. What are you doing as a parent to make your child feel secure in your love?

4. What are some sacrifices you have made for your children that reveal the unconditional nature of your love for them?

A PERSONAL WORD
Thou Shalt Model Godliness

Fashion models stroll down a runway as someone describes the designer's creations they're wearing. As parents, we walk down a runway <u>daily</u> as our children watch. Do they see the Designer's handiwork in our lives?

—E. Y.

Commandment 3

THOU SHALT MODEL GODLINESS

Parents who really love their children provide them with a clear example of how a person should live. Let's face it, something will mold and shape our children. If it's not us, what or who will it be? So as parents, we need to ask two questions:

- What forces mold my children?
- What methods will I use to shape them?

More than three hundred years before the birth of Christ, Plato pondered the importance of the influences on children:

> And shall we just carelessly allow children to hear any casual tale which may be devised by casual persons, and to receive into their minds ideas for the most part the very opposite of those which we wish them to have when they are grown up?
>
> We cannot.

. . . Anything [children receive] into [the] mind at that age is likely to become indelible and unalterable; and therefore it is most important that the tales which the young first hear should be models of virtuous thought.[1]

"Casual persons" represent the forces in society that shape our children by default. By contrast, we parents are to be *intentional* in our commitment to mold our children. All too often, the "casual" powers in culture may be intentional, too. That is, they may be committed to propagandizing the young for their beliefs, values, causes, and products. But they are also "casual" because these powers are people, institutions, and ideas our kids bump up against as they grow up. The "casual" influences are those capricious molders and shapers that don't care whether our children are destroyed or not.

FORCES MOLDING OUR CHILDREN

The Impact of Culture

Again, we must ask ourselves: *What forces mold my children?* The answer is: There are many. First is *the culture itself*. Exactly what is "the culture"? Culture is the outward manifestation of the way people believe. In other words, it's the way a society expresses its fundamental beliefs. Music, graphic arts, books, magazines, movies, television, plays, and sculpture are all elements of culture. What happens when a critical mass of people in a society changes the foundational belief system? The culture will change.

In the twenty-first century, we see a dramatically different culture from the one in which most of us were raised. In fact, some observers of modern society say we live in a "toxic culture." After America was shocked with the horror of the shootings at Columbine High School in Colorado, fifty-six high-profile people, including William Bennett and former

President Jimmy Carter, signed an "Appeal to Hollywood." The signers expressed their concern over "an increasingly toxic popular culture" and called on filmmakers to police themselves.[2]

I once saw a drawing of a demon crawling inside a section of cable when it connected to a house. As the demonic presence inched inside the home, the artist depicted him smiling more and more. If we see the evil aspects of culture as an invasion every bit as spiritually, mentally, and emotionally destructive as a physical home invasion by thugs, we will be much more alert to what our children watch and hear. Sadly, many of us invite in these home invaders!

Impact of Peers

A second force molding our children consists of their peers. Many parents have watched with a desperate sense of helplessness as their children rely less and less on them and more and more on their friends for moral decision-making. This is especially true in the early teen years, when we see our kids leaving the solid mooring of a good home and venturing out on the turbulent sea of peer influence.

Ohio State University researcher Sung Joon Jang found that peer pressure makes its greatest impact around ages thirteen and fourteen. "That's really the entrance to the teen years," said Jang. At that point, "many adolescents are trying to detach themselves from their parents and become more independent." Jang concluded that this early teen period is when "peers suddenly have a very significant role for adolescents."[3]

Peer pressure, for example, is a major cause of teenage sexual activity. A 2003 survey by the Kaiser Family Foundation revealed that boys are pressured by their male friends to have sex with girls. "There are a lot of expectations for boys to be sexually active," reported Julia Davis of the Kaiser Foundation.[4]

The survey also found that both male and female teens reported peer pressure was high regarding drug and alcohol use.

Impact of School Environment

A third force impacting our children is *the school, or educational system*. It's in this environment that peer pressure becomes intense. When you combine the impact of young people's schoolmates with the moral and philosophical drift of modern public education, schools become the strongest, and potentially most harmful, "casual" shapers of children.

What makes this so dangerous is the assumption by many opinion-makers that, because public education is mandatory, the final authority regarding children's schooling does not belong to parents. Thankfully, the Supreme Court rejected this idea when it ruled in 1972, in *Wisconsin v. Yoder*, that Amish parents weren't required to keep their children in school after the eighth grade.

However, in his dissenting opinion back in 1972, Justice William Douglas revealed an educational philosophy that has gained wider acceptance in the judicial establishment. Douglas wrote that though parents would "normally speak for the entire family, the education of a child is a matter on which the child will have decided views." So, according to Douglas, says Stephen L. Carter, "parents who choose a religious education for their children are involved in conduct that is somehow suspect, that the state therefore needs to be a monitor to ensure that the child's wishes are being protected."[5]

If parents don't mold their children, "casual" forces will.

THE QUESTION EVERY PARENT MUST ANSWER

That brings us to the second question we should ask ourselves as parents: *What methods will I use to shape my children?*

There are all kinds of ideas out there. They range from the authoritarian to the laissez-faire. Militant parents use intimidation, condemnation, and domination as if there were no other techniques of molding children's behaviors. Then there are the manipulators. B. F. Skinner summoned parents to "operant conditioning," whereby desired behaviors are reinforced through methods of stark control. Followers of Benjamin Spock, on the other hand, embraced a laissez-faire approach in which the child is allowed to follow his own way. After all, said Jean-Jacques Rousseau way back in the days of revolutionary France, the child is a *tabula rasa*, a "blank slate," and should be allowed to grow up in a "state of nature," where there is "purity."

But I think psychologist and author Carl Pickhardt had it right when he declared, "The power of parental influence comes to this: the example parents model (who and how they are) and the treatment parents give (how they choose to act and react with their child)."[6]

As parents, there are times we have to use direct, confrontational styles of molding our children, including spanking. (Yes, I said spanking. We'll deal with it in a later chapter.) At other times we can allow our children to "settle" into the molds we've made, giving them more freedom. But always, the parent must model the example.

ALWAYS MODEL

Let me add a third question for parents, and I believe it's the most important of all: *What lifestyle will I model for my children?* Moms and dads, your children will do what you say for a while, but then they will do what you do. Or, to paraphrase a comedian of another era, "What *they* see is what *you* get." The example we set for our children serves as a road map as they choose the direction of their own lives. We're all likely to see our beliefs and behaviors popping up in our kids somewhere down the line.

On April 23, 2003, Jack Osbourne, teenage son of rocker Ozzy Osbourne, checked himself into a hospital in Pasadena, California, to deal with a growing problem of drug and alcohol abuse. The power of parental influence was apparently exerted with vigor in the life of this seventeen-year-old. Jack's father opened the second season of the family's hit "reality" TV show, *The Osbournes,* according to an Associated Press report, "boozing heavily to cope with (his wife) Sharon's diagnosis of colon cancer."[7]

A MODEL OF MODELING

By now you understand the importance of our third commandment: *Thou shalt model godliness.* For a model of what modeling godliness means, let's look at the parents of one of ancient Israel's heavy hitters, the prophet Samuel. Samuel was an influential man in his day, both spiritually and politically. He remains a genuine hero of the Bible. What kind of parents did he have?

We meet Samuel's parents in the book of 1 Samuel, right at the beginning. Samuel's mom was Hannah, and his dad was Elkanah. Back in those days, many men had more than one wife. The Bible tells us that when Elkanah offered his sacrifice, he gave some portions to Peninnah, one of his spouses, and to her sons. However, Elkanah would present Hannah a double portion of the sacrifice, because he loved her most of all. But there were no sons to share Hannah's bounty because "the Lord had closed her womb" (1 Samuel 1:4–5).

Let Them See Your Affection

Here's the first lesson we learn if we want to model a positive example for our children: *Parents must love one another and let their children see them expressing affection.* When our sons were growing up, Jo Beth and I wanted them to see that their mom and dad not only loved them but they also loved each other very much. So we made a point to show a proper level of affection to one another in front of the boys. We didn't have to fake it—and you can't fake it either! When Elkanah initially was giving Hannah the double portion, Samuel was not yet around to see it. But you can be certain this was a pattern in the relationship between Elkanah and Hannah, well established by the time Samuel came along. He had many opportunities to see how much his dad loved his mom.

Samuel finally did come into the world—and he did so because of prayer. Remember that Hannah couldn't conceive, so she and Elkanah prayed and prayed. They persisted in going to the altar and making sacrifices and asking godly people to pray for them. Year after year passed, and it seemed their prayers weren't getting through. At last, Hannah began to have those clues she was pregnant, and a few months later, she gave birth to a son—Samuel.

God's Strategic Timing

God's timing may not match ours. Certainly Hannah and Elkanah wanted their baby boy much sooner than God answered their prayers, but they had to wait on His timing. If Samuel had been born earlier, he probably would have been just another kid, skipping rocks, teasing girls, and growing up to be a good but not notable man. But Samuel was born in God's perfect plan at the right place and right time. God answered Hannah's and Elkanah's prayers better than they could have dreamed, though not according to the calendar they would have preferred. How many times in my own life has God answered my prayers later so He could answer them better!

After waiting so long, Elkanah and Hannah lavished love on their son. They showed that love in a special way, described in 1 Samuel 1:21–22:

Then the man Elkanah went up with all his household to offer to the Lord the yearly sacrifice and pay his vow. But Hannah did not go up, for she said to her husband, "I will not go up until the child is weaned; then I will bring him, that he may appear before the Lord and stay there forever."

This provides us with a second great truth we can learn from Elkanah and Hannah: We show our love for our children *by shaping them to live always within the will of God.*

DNA is that all-important biochemical combination that determines our form and being. There is also spiritual DNA that will shape us in relation to God. Elkanah and Hannah wanted Samuel to grow into the man God had intended him to be. They recognized their stewardship, and not only gave him their biological life, but seeded Samuel with the spiritual DNA that would determine his destiny in God's kingdom.

PARENTS AS STEWARDS

Parents who take seriously their role as models for their children understand the stewardship principle. A steward is the manager of someone else's property. In raising their kids, these "steward-parents" know they report to a Higher Authority—the Owner, the Creator Himself. "Possessive parents" fail to see this truth. They feel they "own" their children. They have the attitude they can do anything they want with them—from giving them silly names and dressing them oddly to harming them physically and emotionally.

Other parents delegate the raising of their children. These are the mothers and fathers who allow their children to come under the "casual" influences noted at the beginning of this chapter. "Delegating parents" play the blame-game because they give away their stewardship responsibilities. If their children aren't learning, it's the school's fault. If their children don't have faith, it's the church's fault. If their kids act out what they see on television, it's the entertainment industry's fault. Delegating parents just keep on passing the blame and the buck down the line. And if, as adults, the children fail to measure up to the parents' dreams, delegating parents blame all the forces they allowed to shape their children and usually accept no personal responsibility for the outcome.

Hannah and Elkanah are great examples of parents as stewards. They knew Samuel belonged to God, and that God had entrusted Samuel to them. And they took responsibility for God's property—Samuel. That's still the way God works today. God gives our children to us, but He retains ownership. Our mission as parents is to be stewards—to take care of God's property in this world. That means we must model godliness before our children.

WELL-ESTABLISHED CHARACTER

Hannah and Elkanah, understanding their stewardship as parents, sought to lead Samuel by example. This was because their own characters were well established before Samuel was born. The loving attitude between Elkanah and Hannah prior to Samuel's birth, and their loving behavior continued throughout his childhood and beyond.

It's just as important for moms and dads *as individuals* to cultivate a solid, consistently positive character. Hannah's high character is seen as she dedicates her son to God and sings a beautiful song in which she praises God, who "keeps the feet of His godly ones" (1 Samuel 2:9).

Remember, Hannah and Elkanah did not begin developing their character and building a loving environment *after* Samuel arrived on the scene. This was the atmosphere into which he was born. It's playing catch-up to try to develop such a spiritual and emotional environment when our children are older and things have begun to fall apart. It's hard to change the atmosphere of a home.

Throughout his childhood, Samuel saw Hannah and Elkanah model godliness. He saw the love his parents had for each other. He felt the love his parents had for him as they encouraged him to live always within the will of God. And he witnessed the love they had for God as they dedicated him to the Lord's service.

A while back, before our whole congregation, I decided to test how Jo Beth and I had fared in setting an example for our sons and creating an environment of love and positive character in our home. I invited our boys—all grown with their own families—to sit with me and chat about our family as thousands of people watched. There was some good advice for modeling godliness scattered throughout the interview. It's too lengthy to present in its entirety, but let me share some of the material we covered.

MY THREE SONS

Cliff, our youngest, is founder and lead singer of the Christian music group *Caedmon's Call*. Cliff was named after my good friend Cliff Barrows, who for years has served as worship leader for Billy Graham. So it's fitting that our youngest son turned out to be the musician of the family. When I asked him what he would say to parents wanting to model godliness for their children, Cliff replied, "So many times today you see parents trying to tell their children what godliness is and telling them the difference between wrong and right, but the parents don't live out that godliness themselves." Thankfully, Cliff told me, "The main thing you and mom did so well with us was actually to model godliness."

Cliff also addressed the important matter of parents allowing their children the freedom to settle into the "mold" the mother and father have created. "Parents sometimes seek to make all the decisions for their children and not allow them the opportunity to grow in their own relationships with the

Lord." He reminded me that when he and his brothers were growing up, "You didn't try to tell us what to do all the time, but gave us guidance in how to seek the Lord for answers so we could grow in our relationship to Him."

A Scary Maneuver

Honestly, that's a scary maneuver for us parents. It's like telling our kids to watch how we walk out on a tightwire, then inviting them to follow in our precise steps. The protective instinct makes us want to leave the children on the secure platform while we do the balancing act for them. But there comes a moment when our kids have to step out onto the wire. Their safety is in observing how we have stayed balanced on the wire, and then walking in the same way. As he and his brothers were making their own decisions and cultivating their own relationships with Christ, Cliff noted, "We were watching you and mom and the way you lived your life and handled big decisions."

Ben, our middle son, serves with me in Houston as an associate pastor, overseeing one of the largest singles ministries in the country. Ben reported that people often ask him, "What was it like growing up in a preacher's home, and why aren't you messed up?" When the laughter subsided, Ben confided that things weren't perfect, but he felt he and his brothers didn't fall into radical rebellion because Jo Beth and I sought to maintain a normal home life. "It wasn't like you and mom had this big pulpit Bible beating us over the heads, preaching to us constantly and trying to cram it down our throats. . . . You simply lived it out."

By the way, it's not just preachers who have to overcome the instinct to "preach" to their kids. We all want our children to adopt our value and belief systems. Even the atheist shudders to think of his child becoming a conservative, Bible-believing Christian! The temptation to be "preachy" is especially strong if you're a pastor or Bible teacher. But the balance is found in teaching the children the principles, then modeling them in your daily lifestyle. To return to the tightwire analogy, it's like saying, "Here are the principles of wire-walking. . . . Now watch me do it, and then I want you to do it."

Walking Out on the "Wire"

Ed, our oldest son, is the pastor of a dynamic, cutting-edge church in the Dallas/Fort Worth metroplex. In our interview, he shared that he thought the whole point of parenting is to prepare the children to get out on the "wire" themselves. "I define parenting," he said, "as teaching and training your children to leave home. . . . Parenting is a modeling job."

The teaching plants the truths and principles into the child. The modeling, Ed said, has to do with "authenticity, living life on the rugged plains of reality." He added that it was important that he and his brothers saw Jo Beth and me behave the same away from church as we did at church.

Playing Together and Praying Together

The "when" of parental modeling, then, is every moment, every circumstance. Parents need to give much consideration to the "arena" of modeling—the venues in which they will show their kids important values and principles. Here we come to another one of those balances that keep us upright on the "wire," no matter how strong the winds: playing together *and* praying together.

If I were trying to be pious, I would have put "praying" first in that equation of balance. But *praying* together is much more meaningful if first we have *played* together. Having fun with your children builds the relationship that makes the praying credible and natural for them.

"Our home life," said Cliff, "was not this unbelievably structured, strict, and stiff situation. I remember our home being relaxed." One of Cliff's most pleasant memories, he said, was when he and I played golf and when I attended his sporting events.

IT'S INTENTIONAL, NOT ACCIDENTAL

Believe it or not, we pastors work pretty hard (or at least we should), so like most parents, I had a lot to do. The needs of a church and its membership can consume a lot of time and energy. I had to determine early in my ministry that I would not let those time demands take me away from important events in the lives of our boys. They didn't understand then, but as they grew up and assumed responsibility for their own ministries, they grasped what I was trying to model for them. This lifestyle doesn't happen by accident but by a definite decision and commitment.

"Parents today need to be more intentional, because kids have a lot more distractions than when I was growing up," said Ben. "We need to make sure the TV is not the center of our home life as some kind of electronic baby-sitter."

Resisting culture's propaganda assault on our homes and families happens best when parents prioritize three or four things they are going to do "very well," said Ed. He continued that at the top of that list must be the relationship to God the mother and father have as individuals as well as together. Family life ought to revolve around the church because, in Ed's words, "it's the most important thing going."

The next priority, he thought, must be the couple's marriage. Husbands, he noted, are to love their wives as Christ loved the church, as Paul wrote in Ephesians 5. "In other words," said Ed, "the marriage should take precedence over every other human relationship, including the parent-child relationship." The parent-child relationship grows naturally and spontaneously from the root of the healthy relationship between the father and mother.

THREE ESSENTIALS FOR PARENTAL MODELING

Jo Beth and I sought to model positive principles for our boys through our relationship to one another, as well as to God. In my interview with our three sons, they said kind things about us, but Jo Beth and I both would have to say there were many times we missed the boat. But through the process of raising our sons, there were three important things we learned about modeling godliness before our children.

- Build a lifetime relationship with your mate. Ed has it right—by focusing on your spouse, you are showing your kids what love and family look like. Building such a relationship takes creativity, thoughtfulness, planning, and intentional actions.

- Build a lifetime love affair with your children. Our sons know we love them unconditionally and without bias. No matter what happens, our love for them will not be lessened. And we love them equally. There is no favoritism.

- Most important, build a lifetime love affair with the Lord Jesus Christ. We can preach to our kids until we're blue in the face, but if Jesus Christ is not real in our lives, He won't be in theirs either. Did you know all children have X-ray vision? That's right, they can see right through their parents' hypocrisy. But if you're committed to Christ, X-ray vision is not necessary.

Concerning this last point, your children will get a schooling in how to walk with Christ through life's ups and downs as you live openly in your personal relationship with Christ. Let a vital, healthy relationship with Jesus shine in all you do and say—in the way you love your spouse and through the love you give your children.

THE RESPONSIBILITY IS OURS

Earlier in this chapter, I talked about the influences that come "casually" upon our children. We looked at the "toxic culture" and the people who impact their lives for the worst. But that doesn't mean we are to blame society for what happens to our kids. The onus isn't on TV, music, schools, government, churches, teachers, and all those other "casual" influences. Rather, the responsibility for the way a child is molded and shaped belongs to the parents.

"Why do you love God, son?" a man asked a teenager.

"I don't know," the young man replied, "I guess it just runs in our family."

But it must go deeper than that. Our children need to embrace and internalize biblical faith for themselves. If they don't, they'll be anchorless in the storm of skepticism they may encounter in college or when they are assaulted by the cynicism of unbelieving friends and work associates later in life.

Parents must equip their children to face the tough questions, and, in the words of 1 Peter 3:15, to be able to give a defense for the hope within them. Children need to know that the faith of their parents—and now theirs—is based on fact, rooted in history.

The heart cannot rejoice in what the mind rejects. Some people say, "I believe that it's true." But it's better to be able to declare, "Because it's true, I believe it!" Faith is founded on objective fact. If our children understand that, no one will be able to shake them. Faith resting on the shifting seabed of subjectivism gets washed away with every fresh tide. Objective reality is the rock in which faith is embedded.

Imagine a man trying to cross a frozen river in mid-December. He gets down on his belly and begins to move gingerly out onto the ice. He inches himself along, not wanting to crash through into the frigid waters. He continues to move at a snail's pace. After forty-five minutes, he's made it

71

halfway across. All of a sudden he hears a roar. Here comes a guy riding a snowmobile with a couple of his buddies. They speed down the snowy embankment and out onto the icy river. The ice begins to creak and crack, but they make it to the other side and speed off into the distance.

Now who has more faith—the snow-crawling man or the snowmobile driver? You would have to agree that the snowmobile driver had the greater faith, while the slow-moving, cautious man had little. But the amount of faith is not the decisive factor—they both had the same thick ice. It was the object of their faith that mattered.

Same river a month and a half later: Once again, the man begins his slow crawl across the ice, and once again, here comes the snowmobile. But the ice is thinner now, and it gives way under the man who's crawling and he drowns. The guys on the snowmobile make it a little farther out because of their speed, but they too crash through the ice and perish. The reason they drowned had nothing to do with their faith—the "little bit of faith" drowned and the "lots of faith" drowned. The ice was not thick enough to hold them up. It was both unreliable and unpredictable. It was the object of their faith—the ice—that failed.

How much faith do you have? Jesus said you only need faith the size of a mustard seed and you can move mountains, as long as the object of your faith is Christ—the reliable, unshakable and unbreakable solid Rock.

Certainly as we model faith for our children, it's important that they see the ancient historic facts underlying biblical faith. But the clearest demonstration of the God who operates in the actualities of everyday life is in the exemplary way parents live before their sons and daughters in the here and now. And whether you have a snowmobile amount of faith or a slow crawler amount of faith, your children need to see that the

Rock in which your faith is embedded will never give way beneath you—or beneath them.

And that's why good parenting mandates that fathers and mothers model godliness for their children!

QUESTIONS FOR PARENTS

1. What are some "casual forces" around your children that could exert negative control over them?
2. How is godliness modeled in your home?
3. How is love modeled in your home?
4. Who is the prime influencer in your family?

A PERSONAL WORD
Thou Shalt Teach Thy Children

There are no degrees offered from a "school of parenting." There is no accreditation process for moms and dads . . . but parents are still the best possible teachers for their kids!

Here's a one-chapter course that lays out a curriculum for teaching your kids how to become the godly young men and women you—and the Lord—want them to be.

—E. Y.

THOU SHALT
TEACH THY CHILDREN

Years ago, a poignant television ad for the American Cancer Society depicted a father and his young son together in the den of their home. The ad showed the little boy mimicking every move his father made. When the father sat down in the chair and took off his shoes, his son took off his shoes. When the dad propped up his feet, so did his little boy. When the dad picked up the newspaper, his son picked up a nearby magazine and began reading it, upside down. Then the ad shows the father reaching over to the coffee table and picking up a pack of cigarettes. The dad lit up and began to smoke. The son looked at his father, walked over to where his father was seated and looked down at the pack of cigarettes.

At that moment, you heard the voice of the announcer: "Like father, like son. Think about it."

When it comes to parenting, modeling and teaching go together like peanut butter and jelly. All parents are modeling some type of lifestyle, and all parents are teaching principles, for good or for bad. In the previous chapter we said that what parents must model is godliness. Now the core question is: *What will we teach?*

A friend of mine had a son who, at age seventeen, declared he would "never" be like his dad. Almost twenty years later, the son, now married with three children, laughed as he talked one evening with his father, describing the characteristics he had developed in adulthood. "I suddenly realized the other day, *I have become my dad*," the son chuckled.

PARENTS MUST BE LEARNERS

Parenting carries with it a demand for a brand-new bag of skills. *Along with being teachers, parents have to be learners.* It's only when our children are grown and have their own kids that we get our report cards, discovering just how well we learned—and transferred—parenting skills. In other words, Jo Beth and I see our "grades" whenever we observe our three sons with their children. Thankfully for our sons (and their father), their mother gets an A+!

So our challenge is to teach our children, and teach them well. A mom who really did that effectively is an obscure lady in the Bible named Eunice. Without Dr. Spock, parenting conferences, or books like Dr. Dobson's, Eunice did an outstanding job raising and teaching her son, Timothy. He grew up to become, in God's kingdom, a leader, spokesman, statesman, and church planter.

Clearly, Eunice had a Ph.D. from the university of parenting. Where did she go for her schooling as a mother? Paul gives a clue in a letter to young Timothy: "You, however, continue in the things you have learned and become convinced of, knowing from whom you have learned them; and that from childhood you have known the sacred writings which are able to give you the wisdom that leads to salvation through faith which is in Christ Jesus" (2 Timothy 3:14–15).

Timothy had been trained from his childhood in the "sacred writings." Eunice used the best parenting book ever penned—the Old Testament, containing treasures such as the book of Proverbs. This book is composed of valuable principles stated concisely and without flourish.

A PERFECT TEACHING TOOL: EIGHT PRINCIPLES FROM PROVERBS

These truths about how to live a godly life constitute a perfect tool for teaching children how to live as the Creator intended. Eunice no doubt used these principles to train Timothy and to shape him into the excellent man he became. Along the way, she would have taught him the eight Proverbs principles so valuable in training children.

1. Teach Children Reverence

Principle one is that *all learning must begin with reverence for God.* Timothy probably heard Eunice read the words from Proverbs, "The fear of the Lord is the beginning of knowledge; fools despise wisdom and instruction" (Proverbs 1:7). This biblical truth is the foundation for a wise and godly life, and when it comes to living in peace and joy, that's the only life that matters. "Professor Parent" must start right here, teaching children to "fear," to have a wonder-filled, awed, worshipful reverence for God. Children who grow up with reverence for God will reverence what He has made as well, starting with other people. This is because, as Paul Woodruff writes, reverence "bridges the gap between religious and secular life."[1] Reverence for God carries over into the attitudes and practices of everyday living.

The crises of modern culture have been lamented in sermons, books, songs, poems, reports, policy papers, academic lectures, and political speeches. But there is hardly a problem we and our children face that does not relate back to the loss of the idea of reverence. Abortion on demand and murder result from the loss of reverence for human life. All addictions relate to a person's loss of reverence for himself or herself, resulting in diminished self-respect. Crime comes from a lack of reverence for other people's property. Adultery, fornication, rape, and all forms of sex abuse are the outcomes of a failure to reverence human sexuality. Environmental disasters occur often because of a failure to reverence the Creator's natural handiwork.

Some parents unconsciously teach *irreverence*. Without thinking, they mimic television shows and movies, whose only mention of the word "God" is in a vulgar context. Every time I hear people exclaim, "O my God!" or "O Lord!" or "Jesus!" as a form of cheap slang, I grit my teeth in frustration. The trivializing of "God" or "Lord" is an act of irreverence. To use Christ's name as an expression of surprise or disgust is actually to make it a curse word; it is among the worst of blasphemies because that name brings the greatest of blessing —the opposite of a curse—to the world. When we use God's name, it should be in a prayerful, respectful manner, displaying awe and wonder. We should teach our children that God's names are holy—sacred, set apart, and to be honored (Exodus 20:7).

Raising a human being of knowledge and wisdom is like erecting a building. It all stands on the foundation of reverencing God. Eunice got the point. In fact "Timothy," the name she gave her son, means "fear of God." Begin here, and you will lay the sturdy base for the building up of a healthy, happy human being.

2. Teach Children the Importance of Obedience

Principle two for instructing our children is to *help children learn obedience*. Eunice would have read to Timothy the counsel of Proverbs 1:8: "Hear, my son, your father's instruction, and do not forsake your mother's teaching." This passage shows what complete teaching in a home ought to look like, as well as the distinct roles of the father and mother. The father provides "instruction." In the Hebrew language of the original Proverbs, this referred to authoritative teaching in the form of warnings. Dads have the responsibility of teaching in a way that corrects wrongs and points out the negative consequences of not learning the lessons. Moms provide "teaching." Literally, the term means to "goad." It carries the idea of coaxing someone into good behavior and prodding him in the right direction. Ideally in a healthy family, there's the father with his firm yet temperate stress on the outcomes of ignorance, and the mother with her gentle pushes and shoves toward truth.

Now, we know little about Timothy's father (except he was a Gentile). Perhaps Timothy grew up in a single-parent home. We do know, though, he had a strong grandmother who may have provided the balance of "instruction." God will enable a single parent to fill both roles when necessary. But the ideal environment for training children is the blend of the father's seemingly "heavy" instruction and the mother's nourishing, nudging teaching. In that balance, children best learn obedience.

Growing up under his wise mother, Timothy probably learned more important lessons than the following "Things My Mother Taught Me," recounted by one anonymous writer:

> *My mother taught me logic:* "Because I said so, that's why."
>
> *My mother taught me humor:* "When that lawn mower cuts off your toes, don't come running to me."
>
> *My mother taught me about sex:* "How do you think you got here?"
>
> *My mother taught me about receiving:* "You are going to get it when we get home."

My mother taught me about justice: "One day you'll have kids and I hope they turn out just like you. Then you'll see what it's like."

My mother taught me about religion: "You better pray that'll come out of the carpet."[2]

The older children become, the harder it is to teach them to obey. The obedience lesson has to be sown into the child early in life. Honor and respect for parents is the "kindergarten" of learning obedience. Exodus 20:12 records the first of God's commandments with a promise attached to it: "Honor your father and your mother, that your days may be prolonged in the land which the Lord your God gives you." This command holds the secret to longevity that's better than jogging or eating right—honoring parents. Those who obey receive the resulting promise of being "prolonged" in God's land.

There is a link between principle and practice. Children who learn parental respect at the beginning of life will understand the necessity of obeying sound principles throughout life—and that results in health and well-being. In the Old Testament, the land of promise is a type and symbol of the life of goodness, joy, and peace that God wills for His created beings. But to enjoy those blessings on a sustained basis, we must obey the principles of good living prescribed by the Creator of the universe and "described" in the life-experience of Jesus Christ in His incarnation.

Sadly, many elements of today's toxic culture undermine parental authority and respect. One promoter of contemporary rock music, who had catapulted many performers to stardom, was asked how he did it. "I look for someone their parents will hate," he replied.[3] Driving a wedge between parents and children may be the launchpad for the short term, meteoric rise to rock music fame, but it is deadly to sustaining quality living over the long term.

3. Teach Kids Purity

The third principle is to teach our children *purity.* The evidence is that Eunice and Lois (Timothy's grandmother) were strong, straight-spoken women who were leaders. Doubtless one of them, perhaps both, taught Timothy how Solomon urged his own son to seek wisdom so he would be delivered from sexual impurity (see Proverbs 2:1–19). Solomon told his son (and all of us) that if he would do that, "you will walk in the way of good men, and keep to the paths of the righteous" (Proverbs 2:20).

Internet systems and TV sets these days provide "parental controls" in the form of advanced technologies, including software (the so-called "V chips") that block certain content. There is also a rating system for CDs and video games, which should be enforced at the store. But the best "parental controls" are still the parents. We need to be the "filter" that protects our children's eyes, ears, and hearts from the violence and sexual immorality so prevalent in our society.

Moms and dads must agree on and set boundaries for their children when it comes to the media. These boundaries need to be both quantitative and qualitative. That is, there should be limitations on how much time a child can spend in front of the TV or computer, or listening to music. Safeguards also must be established regarding content. In other words, it's not in your ten-year-old's best interest to attend an R-rated movie, even if he argues he's the only ten-year-old inhabiting planet Earth who hasn't seen it yet.

Now, let me warn you. Monitoring the media in your home and in your child's life will take work. Especially when you consider that the average American home reportedly has three TV sets, two VCRs, three radios, three tape players, two CD players, a video game system, and one personal computer. So you may feel a bit stretched to oversee your child's use of all those gadgets, but the caring parent who wants to teach purity to his or her child will find a way!

Whatever else it is, that "way" will involve the parents' time and participation. If you allow video games, play them with your children. Watch movies and TV programs together. Cultivate your children's musical tastes and choices. Oversee computer use rather than sending your child off to a separate room alone to surf the 'Net. In other words, parents committed to teaching their children purity will not succumb to the "get-them-out-of-the-way, get-them-out-of-my-hair, let-them-make-their-own-decisions" parental attitude that's so widespread in our culture.

Many parents don't teach principles of purity because they've lost a vision for the clean and decent through decades of the moral equivalent of "dumbing down." A slow slide into moral deviancy can occur over time. However, there can also be a build-up toward an increasing understanding of purity. The method of teaching children high moral principles can be compared to climbing a ladder.

- *First rung: boundaries* (early through mid-childhood). At this stage, parents must focus on saying no. Children not yet capable of understanding moral principles will understand there are healthy limitations on behavior.

- *Second rung: consequences* (late childhood through mid-adolescence). At this level children can begin to "connect the dots." As children become capable of understanding, parents should teach them about the law of sowing and reaping. They not only must be *told* about the relationship between moral choices and outcomes but also be allowed to *experience* consequences. Sometimes parents will have to pull away the protective hand and let the child deal with the results of wrong behaviors.

- *Third rung: principles* (late adolescence). As children prepare to leave the family nest, parents need to instruct them in the deep truths of moral principles. Through such conversations, mothers and fathers can link all the stages. Boundaries were set early, before there was understanding, because actions and behaviors have consequences; now the child learns that life is not to be lived merely on pragmatics but on eternal principles.

When we take our children up these three rungs, they are able to depart for college, marriage, or the marketplace with the whole picture, understanding why the pure life is important.

4. Teach Children About Money

Such principles and truths are not ethereal and theoretical but deal with the reality of everyday life. So the fourth component in the parental curriculum should be one of the major elements in daily living: *teach your children how to handle money.* "Honor the Lord from your wealth and from the first of all your produce," says Proverbs 3:9. The principle of tithing is that we honor the Lord by giving Him back a portion of what He has given us. Children need to learn this early. In fact, this will be a key to helping them learn how to handle finances responsibly.

By setting aside the "first of all your produce," your family budget has a standard that guides all spending. So if buying a new car threatens our ability to tithe, we need to choose a more affordable vehicle. Responsible financial management always hinges on spending priorities. When God is first in our budget, all other items will be arranged in relation to that top priority. That's among the things Jesus meant when He said in Matthew 6:33 that we are to "seek first" God's kingdom and character, and *"all these things shall be added to you"* (emphasis added).

What constitutes "all these things"? The context of Jesus' remarks explains it.

> For this reason I say to you, do not be worried about your life, as to what you will eat, or what you will drink; nor for your body, as to what you will put on. Is not life more than food, and the body more than clothing? Look at the birds of the air, that they do not sow, nor reap nor gather into barns, and yet your heavenly Father feeds them. Are you not worth much more than they? And who of you by being worried can add a single hour to his life? Do not worry then, saying, "What will we eat?" or "What will we drink?" or "What will we wear for clothing?" For the Gentiles eagerly seek all these things; for your heavenly Father knows that you need all these things (Matthew 6:25–27, 31–32).

Jesus is saying that if God comes first in the stewardship of our material resources, all the other bits and pieces find their proper place!

So we need to teach our children about money—beginning with stewardship. I would suggest starting young children with a small allowance that increases gradually as they grow older. Show them how to allot the portions. Let your child watch you place your offering in the collection plate at church. Then allow him to hold the plate for himself and drop in his gift. Teach the child the importance of saving a fraction of his money.

As children become older, they should be required to plan for and be responsible for certain needs, like favorite clothing items and lunch money. Then tell your children the rest is for personal use—entertainment, toys, and other non-necessary, "fun" things.

One helpful way to teach your children how to allot their money is by using "tithe" as an acrostic:

T = Ten percent. The first 10 percent belongs to God.

I = Interest. Put some money aside so it will earn interest.

T = Today. Jesus taught us to pray, "Give us *today* our daily bread." The "today" element of a budget refers to the essentials for daily living, like food and clothing.

H = Household. Set aside money for expenses relating to the home. (While a child won't be required to pay utilities, he or she does need to understand the cost components of operating a house.)

E = Entertainment. Children need to understand this comes at the bottom, not the top. It's what's left over after the other expenses are met. The child learns not to buy a computer game the moment someone gives him money but to consider the other elements first.

5. Teach a Healthy View of Love

Sadly, what many people learn as they grow up is the love of money and the devaluing of persons. So, the fifth principle is teach your children *to love others.* "Do not withhold good from those to whom it is due, when it is in your power to do it. Do not say to your neighbor, 'Go, and come back, and tomorrow I will give it,' when you have it with you," says Proverbs 3:27–28. The emphasis in this passage is on love as action, and that's what we need to teach our children.

A massive perversion of the concept of love has occurred in the world in which today's children will mature. Love has been reduced to either the physical—the sex act—or to primarily a sentimental emotion. The Bible gives us the healthy view, and this is the style we must relate to our kids. Love may or may not be something you *feel,* but love is something you *do*—for *others.* In the Bible, love is more a verb than a noun. "Greater love has no one than this," Jesus told His followers, "that one lay down his life for his friends" (John 15:13). Parents must teach children the connection between loving and doing.

John Lennon, former Beatle and songwriter, described himself as a socialist. Yet when he died, Lennon had accumulated a fortune of more than $200 million. Theoretically, socialists believe wealth should be distributed and there should be no classes separating people—no rich and poor. So Lennon and many social advocates like him cannot be presented as examples of what they say they believe.

Likewise, there are parents who talk to their children about the importance of love but don't back up their talk with their example. The children watch their parents be rude to waiters, holler at the maid, rip into the auto mechanic, gossip bitterly about aunts, uncles, cousins, and other relatives.

During the era of the resettling in America of refugees from war-torn Southeast Asia (the 1970s and early 1980s), a family accepted responsibility for a Cambodian mother and her three children. The Asian children had seen their father brutally murdered by the Khmer Rouge. The American children watched as their parents gave the Cambodian refugees the hospitality of their home. Working together, the members of the American family helped clothe the Cambodian mother and her children, train the mother for a job, and assist the refugee children in starting to school. Today the Cambodian children have become successful professional people. The American kids have become experts in something else—how to love people genuinely.

6. Teach Control of the Tongue

The sixth principle parents must teach their children is *how to control the tongue.* Proverbs 4:24 counsels us to "put away . . . a deceitful mouth and put devious speech far from you."

Literally, "deceitful" describes what is distorted or crooked. Today, we talk about "spin," or a particular interpretation favorable to an individual, especially as it relates to politics.

But we also teach our children to be "spin doctors" when we allow them to put an intentional twist on what they seek to communicate. Far too often our children learn how to "spin" the truth from our example as we exaggerate, make false claims, and spread rumors. If we want to teach our children to communicate without distorting facts, then we must set the example through forthright interactions with them and allow them to listen to us talk honestly with others.

The second phrase in Proverbs 4:24, "devious speech," comes from a Hebrew term meaning to "turn aside" or "depart." Here's the picture of a communication someone has to whisper or speak outside the hearing of those affected. Gossip is one form of devious speech. So is spreading rumors, half-truths, and lies about people. Children should be taught that if they have to whisper a "secret" about someone, then it's best left unsaid.

On the positive side, parents should teach their children the value of edifying speech. The Bible says we are to "encourage . . . and build up one another (1 Thessalonians 5:11). We are to let our speech "always be with grace, as though seasoned with salt, so that you will know how you should respond to each person" (Colossians 4:6). This means parents should focus on helping their children develop a positive vocabulary, full of words that bless others. Parents must also teach their children propriety in communicating. That means they learn what is suitable in speech and conversation and what is not.

Not only do we need to teach our children about speaking appropriately, we need to be an example of appropriate speech ourselves. Sometimes we parents learn that the hard way—as when the pastor comes visiting and your little girl proclaims, "My mommy says she looks forward to your sermons so she can get a nap before she has to go home and feed us lunch." Or when your boss is invited for a meal, and your son asks, "Can I feel your head? My daddy says you have the hardest head of anybody he's ever worked for!" Some conversation is simply not suitable. We need to help our children know the difference.

7. Teach Your Children to Work

The seventh principle is teach your children a *strong work ethic*. "How long will you lie down, O sluggard? When will you arise from your sleep?" asks Proverbs 6:9. The passage continues with a warning: "A little sleep, a little slumber, a little folding of the hands to rest—your poverty will come in like a vagabond and your need like an armed man" (vv. 10–11).

Children need to learn how to work and how to be accountable. The best way to do this is by giving our children chores. We need to lay out the expectations about how the work is to be done and then come back to evaluate how well the child did the assigned task. This prepares our children for working in the marketplace with its missions, goals, objectives, job descriptions, action plans, and annual reviews.

The boy or girl who is never given responsibility never learns to be responsible. Children who never have to measure up to expectations in the performance of a task fail to learn the importance of meeting and exceeding a boss's requirements. Those youngsters whose parents require no accountability for execution of a task won't be accountable. We teach our children a good work ethic when we give them responsibility, lay out the expectations, and demand accountability.

8. Teach About Choosing Godly Friends

The eighth principle is teach your children *how to select good, godly friends*. Proverbs 13:20 says, "He who walks with wise men will be wise, but the companion of fools will suffer harm."

In 1936, Jesse Owens, a gifted African-American athlete,

represented the United States in the Olympic Games. That year, the games were held in Berlin, and Adolph Hitler himself had attended the opening ceremony. Owens seemed a sure bet to win the long jump. As he practiced, however, he noticed a slender, athletic German getting in some very long practice jumps. Owens tensed as he thought of the Nazi desire to show "Aryan superiority," especially over a black person.

Unexpectedly, the German walked over and spoke to Owens, introducing himself as Luz Long. Owens was amazed as Long encouraged him and made suggestions on how Owens could jump even farther. Jesse Owens did exactly that, setting an Olympic record and winning the gold medal in the event. Luz Long—in front of Hitler—publicly congratulated Owens. "You could melt down all the medals and cups I have," Owens said later, "and they wouldn't be a plating on the 24-carat friendship I felt for Luz Long."[4]

One of the most effective ways we can teach our children to choose friends is by helping them develop a profile of a true friend. Certainly it would include the fact that friends are people—like Luz Long—who encourage and help us do our best. But the best way we can help them develop a true friend profile is by studying with them the friendship model of Jesus. Those who obey Him, Jesus said, are His friends (John 15:14). Jesus shows that a friend is someone who will sacrifice for another (John 15:13). As our children get a clear picture of friendship, they are able to discern the difference between friends and mere associates.

A LEARNING ENVIRONMENT

Once, the core of a good education was considered to be "reading, writing, and arithmetic." Before that, the ideal curriculum would have included philosophy, theology, the ancient classics, geography, and science. But no matter how great the curriculum, if the context—the delivery system and environment—is not right, the pupil will not learn.

Young Timothy studied in the proper context. Paul tells us in 2 Timothy 1:5 there was a "sincere faith" that characterized Eunice and Lois. The lessons they taught Timothy were not the drivel from a dry textbook or some irrelevant theory. The lessons they taught were from the overflow of their rich lives. Their methodology was to live before Timothy their own deep relationship with Jesus Christ. Perhaps they followed Jesus' model of teaching through parables to which Timothy could relate. As Eunice and Lois spun the stories and made the applications, Timothy saw their own excellent character and understood their instruction as living principles.

Perhaps the greatest lesson we learn from Timothy, Lois, and Eunice is that our homes are the most important schools our children will ever attend, and we are the most important teachers our kids will ever have. When we realize this, we will raise children who don't just have information, but wisdom for living.

QUESTIONS FOR PARENTS

1. What are some areas of parenting in which you need to be a learner?
2. What elements of a child's education should be the priority of the home?
3. Who was the best teacher you ever had and what made that person so effective?
4. How does each of your children learn best?

A PERSONAL WORD
Thou Shalt Spend Time with Thy Children

How do your kids know you love them?

"Cause I tell them so."

Not good enough, mom and dad. This chapter gives you tried and true principles for giving your children what they need from you most.

"Love?"

Yes, in the form of your time.

—E. Y.

Commandment 5

THOU SHALT SPEND TIME WITH THY CHILDREN

How can you deal with a parent who never wants to spend time with you? She comes home from work, fixes herself dinner, and stays in her room sleeping and watching TV the rest of the night. When I come in to talk to her, she gets mad at me."

This was one of many notes penned by youth who attend our church's annual beach retreat. Every summer, I'm privileged to accompany more than one thousand junior-high and high-school students on these weeklong excursions into fun and spiritual growth. During the week, we ask the kids to write down statements or questions about their home or parents.

One of our junior high students responded to a question asked on one of these retreats. The question was, "If a book were written about your family, what would the title be?" His answer speaks volumes: *Hi, Dad. Bye, Dad.*

These two young people voice the heartache of so many children and teens who yearn for quality time with their parents. Children equate love with time. In fact, if you were to ask kids how to spell "love," they would answer T-I-M-E.

DEBUNKING THE OLD MYTH

There's an old myth still being articulated by parents today: "I may not spend quantity time with my kids, but I give them quality time." The truth is it has to be quantity *and* quality time. The equation of love won't balance any other way. Our children recognize their importance to us by the amount of time we spend with them. In budgeting time, our children must be near the top.

David was an example of a man who didn't know where to place his children among his priorities. In terms of wanting to please the Lord, David was a man "after [God's] own heart" (1 Samuel 13:14; Acts 13:22). Israel's shepherd-king was a military genius, successful monarch, musician, and talented poet. He was a prodigy. Yet his children's lives had disastrous outcomes. How could this have happened? No doubt David's kids inherited some of his giftedness and grew up in the plush comfort of the king's palace. Yet their lives ended in tragedy.

The Bible says we "all have sinned" (Romans 3:23), and David certainly proves the point. As a result of his adulterous affair with Bathsheba, David arranged for the death of her husband, Uriah. And God's judgment followed—the sword would never leave David's household (see 2 Samuel 12:10). Certainly that consequence affected David's children, yet it doesn't explain totally what happened to his offspring.

The experience of three of David's children, Absalom, Tamar, and Amnon, as recorded in 2 Samuel 13, gives us a clue. Amnon was the half-brother of Tamar and Absalom and was crazed with a crush on Tamar, who was stunningly beautiful. Amnon craved her so passionately it made him sick. With a friend, he hatched a plot to rape her, and David, oblivious to what was happening in his own household, became a pawn in the plan.

Amnon put on a believable sick-act and asked his father the king to send Tamar to take care of him. When Tamar showed up, Amnon violated her. David found out what happened and—did nothing at all (2 Samuel 13:21). The requirements of God's Law were clear: Amnon should have been executed. But because he was David's own son, the king could not bring himself to carry out the punishment.

RELENTLESS ANGER

Absalom had no such reservations. Since his father the king did nothing, he would do something. Though he waited two years, Absalom avenged his sister, Tamar, by arranging the murder of Amnon. Then, afraid of David's wrath, Absalom fled. He lived in exile in Geshur for three years, away from his dad. But David's heart yearned for his son, and he brought Absalom back to Jerusalem. Yet David couldn't let go of his anger totally, so he prohibited Absalom from seeing his face.

Two more years passed, and finally Absalom was allowed into David's presence. Five years a half decade—of seething, volcanic anger in Absalom over the rape of his sister, the sly betrayal by his half-brother, and rejection by his father had hardened like lava turned into stone. Absalom's heart turned against his father, David, and he plotted the king's overthrow. Now it was David's turn to flee Absalom. The son moved quickly into the power-vacuum left by the father. As if that were not enough, Absalom organized a posse to pursue David.

As a young man, David had been forced to flee King Saul. Now, in his later life, David was running from his own son.

David sent out his forces to meet Absalom and his army. He told his generals to go easy on his son, and not to harm him. He still hoped for reconciliation and healing of the relationship.

However, Joab, a fierce warrior at David's side, ignored the command. He killed Absalom.

The cry of David's anguish haunts history: "O my son Absalom, my son, my son Absalom! Would I had died instead of you, O Absalom, my son, my son!" (2 Samuel 18:33). Death would have been a caressing touch to David's wounded soul, but it would not come and free him from the hurt that had devastated his family and personal life.

Five years of neglect—and who can say how many more? —had taken their toll. *David was willing to give his life for his son, but he would not give him his time.*

Maybe David's children felt like the youngster I heard about whose father operated like a drill sergeant. Every morning after breakfast he would muster the kids in a rigidly straight line for inspection to make sure teeth were brushed, noses were clean, hair was in place, ears washed, and shirts pressed and tucked. After this inspection would come the orders for the day. Finally, the man's youngest son would have no more of it. When the sergeant-father came to the little boy one day in the inspection, the youngster eyeballed him and said, "Sir, is there any way I can transfer out of this 'chicken' outfit?"

BE A *PAL*

David's children might have asked the same question. Despite all his vast material resources and giftedness, David was not a friend to his sons and daughters. True, some parents take it too far. Like the mother who lives vicariously through her cheerleader daughter, or the dad who delights in and encourages his son's wild oats sowing. Children need fathers and mothers, not parents trying to be their peers.

Rather than a peer-friendship from the parents, children need a "PAL"-friendship. A healthy PAL friendship looks like this:

P = Parents are *present*.
A = Parents are *available*.
L = Parents are *listening*.

David's household would have had a different atmosphere and outcome had he been a "PAL" to his children.

BE A PRESENT *PAL*

About Scheduled Time

To be present with our kids, we must schedule time with them. In some ways, the late Bob Pierce was a hero of the faith. He also illustrates the need for parents to have a consistent presence with their children. Traveling in Korea after the war there, his missionary heart was moved over the suffering of the people—especially the children. Bob Pierce vowed to do something about it. He spent years circling the globe, building the international ministry that would be known as World Vision.

But in the process, Bob had to leave his family over large stretches of time, sometimes as long as ten months. Marilee Pierce Dunker, Bob's daughter, wrote a book about growing up with Bob as a father, entitled *Days of Glory, Seasons of Night*. She described the philosophy that guided Bob Pierce: "I've made an agreement with God that I'll take care of his helpless little lambs overseas if He'll take care of mine at home."

Many of us make covenants claiming God as a partner when in reality He has no part of it. Such was apparently the case with Bob. One of his children committed suicide, Bob lost his marriage, and he went through a lonely passage to death.

Maybe God wouldn't be Bob's covenant partner regarding his family because God's Word says, "If anyone does not provide for his own, and especially for those of his household, he has denied the faith, and is worse than an unbeliever" (1 Timothy 5:8). No doubt Bob was a good provider when it came to the material needs of his family. But, by the witness of his daughter, he failed to provide the greatest of their needs—his presence in the form of time spent with them.

Children need to experience a daily presence from their parents. True, some mothers and fathers have jobs that require travel. But it's vital even under those circumstances to "presence" with the kids, whether it's by frequent phone calls, E-mails, or other communications targeted for individual children in the family. The message must be conveyed that the highest priority in a parent's daily family schedule is the child.

Taking Advantage of Serendipity

In the midst of scheduled time, we parents should not forget to be spontaneous. Serendipity is wonderful for those fun things that "just happen." Every family needs surprises and spontaneity. It's great when dad comes home and says, "Let's go get a pizza!" Kids really enjoy it when mom, without any forewarning, announces a picnic.

Of course, we should not rely on serendipity for the entire relational schedule. Serendipity must be balanced by *scheduled time*—intentional, planned interactions between parents and children. Meals, praying together, bedtime, games, reading—all should be planned so they become teaching, conversational, and relationship-building opportunities.

Cal Ripken, future baseball Hall of Famer, said the best advice he ever heard about being a father was the idea that each child is a blank tape constantly running and recording information. The teammate who shared the advice asked Cal, "Whose information do you want on that tape?" With his steel-blue eyes, Cal answered, "My information!"

Input is the means by which information gets on a tape. Far too many parents fail to schedule "recording sessions" with their children. Because they have no time for presence with their kids, moms and dads become little more than background noise on the tape of their children's lives. And I've discovered that kids are very skilled at screening out background noise and focusing on what *they* feel to be important.

Including Spectator Time

A second type of parental time involvement with children is *spectator time*. Our children need us to watch them execute talents and abilities and applaud their accomplishments. Timmy loved to swim. Whenever his father would take him to the neighborhood pool, he would shout, "Daddy, watch what I can do!" Then Timmy would hop off the side of the pool with an awkward, uncoordinated splash. In his mind, Timmy was as polished as any Olympic diver. Timmy's dad failed to understand his little boy was seeking approval and respect from the most important man in his life, so he barely looked up from the book he was reading or work he was doing at poolside. The father didn't have a clue how much his son needed him to watch as he jumped into the pool and to cheer for his achievement.

When Timmy grew up, he was obnoxious and overbearing. He always wanted to be the center of attention. The truth was he was a man who had been starved of spectator time. That lack of healthy emotional nurture impacted his behavior as an adult as much as being deprived of food would have limited his physical development.

Among the first things I've told every congregation that I've pastored is that my children would have proper priority in my scheduling. They understood that this was so important to me that if one of my sons had a game during a time I was supposed to be in the pulpit, I would attend his game. They could always get a substitute preacher, but my boys couldn't get a substitute dad. That may sound like an extreme decision, but extraordinary efforts demonstrate to our children just how significant they are.

Including Special Time

A third opportunity to be present with our children comes during *special times*. Life flows in a set routine for most families, rushing along inside the carefully defined channels of work, school, homemaking, church, sports, music lessons, and sleep. Special times are like great open bays that suddenly widen the narrow channel, providing pleasant interludes in the midst of the routine. They include family vacations, camping trips, theme park jaunts, or attendance at a special event.

It's the special times that make memories lasting—those fun family stories that get told and retold. Jo Beth and I love being with our sons and their families. Rarely do we gather that one of the boys won't say, "Mom and Dad, remember that time when we . . . ?" What follows is family treasure.

Parents must be intentional about special times. Look at your family calendar and schedule and plan occasions that will go in your memory books. Some families schedule special times on a quarterly basis, and others monthly. There can even be weekly special times, such as going out to a family movie, favorite pizza place, or local park.

BE AN AVAILABLE *PAL*

About Unscheduled Time

In addition to scheduled times, there are also *unscheduled times*. That brings us to the "A" in our PAL acronym: *availability*. Children don't always operate on our carefully planned, intricately detailed, intentionalized schedules. In fact, some unwritten law of nature must exist, stipulating that kids will approach their parents with life's deepest philosophical questions at the most inconvenient moments! Rather than being frustrated, however, we need to see these "interruptions" as prime opportunities to show our children we're willing to drop everything to be available to them.

Keeping a Healthy Focus

It's also true that children must be taught when not to interrupt, nor to expect parents always to respond to every whim. We must give our children a proper focus and avoid the extremes of either spoiling or ignoring them.

Imagine that your boss comes in one day and says, "This project is vital to our company, and that's why I'm giving it to you." In one stroke the boss has complimented you and created more tension for you. You labor at the fine points of the project and come to issues only the boss can answer. So, you go through the proper channels and call his secretary. You tell her you really need to see the boss because you need answers concerning the project he has assigned to you.

She puts you on hold, then returns. "I'm sorry, but the earliest he can see you is two weeks from today."

"But the questions I have are essential to completing the project and only he can give me the answers," you protest.

"Hold, please," she replies. You thump your desk and rattle papers as the phone system's background music drones.

After a few suffocating moments, she is back on the line. "I'm sorry, but two weeks is the absolute earliest he can see you." As you hang up the phone, you sink into the awareness that the project's really not that important after all.

Now, put yourself in your children's shoes. When they come to you with what they consider urgent problems and you don't give them—literally—the time of day, they too will sink into the abyss of insignificance. They conclude that the questions gnawing at their minds or the problems burning a hole in their souls are not important enough to you. Or worse yet, they conclude that they themselves are not important enough.

Doing a Priority Review

Every parent needs to do a regular priority review. We are all in multiple roles, each with its own set of demands and priorities. Periodically, we all need to sit down with the Lord through prayer and His Word and ask ourselves, *What demands on my time have eternal significance?*

Those are the ones that merit your top attention and effort.

In a previous chapter we talked about Jesus' one criteria for priority-setting with respect to money. His mandate to seek first God's kingdom applies to our prioritization of time as well. Remember, He said if we would use the kingdom as our sole standard of determining what's important, all these "other things" would be added in (Matthew 6:33).

The problem with many of us in vocational Christian service is we mistake the identity of the interests of the kingdom. We think it's the church or movement we lead or serve, when in reality it's family. The original institution set apart by God to advance His kingdom interests in the world was the family. Being available to your children in those unscheduled times is one of the most important facets of getting that priority right.

When our boys were growing up, it seemed to me they always wanted to talk late on Saturday nights. Now, delivering sermons weekly is like a college student having a term paper to present every seven days, or a Ph.D. candidate facing a roomful of academics for an oral exam. My Saturday nights were intense as I put on the finishing touches and readied to face the congregation in a few short hours.

One Saturday night when Ed was just a little guy, he zipped into our room and started talking like a sputtering jet. Finally I said, "Son, I've got work to do tonight, and then I have to get up early and work some more in the morning. Daddy has to preach tomorrow! So you go on to bed and let me finish this work, and we'll talk another time, okay?" I can still see him scampering back to his room.

"We'd Better Listen"

I felt I had resolved the situation satisfactorily; that is, until Jo Beth spoke up. "Edwin, when they want to talk, whenever it is, I think we'd better listen."

Jo Beth was right. (She usually is.) Since that evening, there have been many Saturday nights when I wondered how I would get my work finished and whether I would be sharp in the pulpit or a mumbling minister trying to stay awake through his own sermon. But it didn't matter; I determined to be available to my boys. Throughout the years my sons and I have talked about dating, peer pressure, temptation, and all the other topics surrounding adolescence. Jo Beth and I simply came to a decision that we would be available—period. Parents must extend to their children an open door, open heart, and open agenda. Don't give your children a constant busy signal. Let them know you are available.

Kurt Warner, once named the Most Valuable Player in the National Football League, is one of the most gifted quarterbacks in professional football. This Super Bowl champion is also a committed follower of Jesus Christ. When his team, the St. Louis Rams, won their conference championship game on the road to the Super Bowl, there was a huge celebration. The party's organizers wanted all the team members to be present. You can imagine the disappointment when Warner turned down the invitation.

"I'm sorry, guys," he said. "I can't be part of your celebration because I promised my family I would be home with them."

That night, Kurt Warner sat down to pizza with his wife and kids. The children gave him a card decorated with the Rams' blue and gold colors and bunches of little hearts. The

103

card read, "You're as Great a Dad as You are a Quarterback."[1] Kurt Warner's children knew they fit at the top of their father's priority list because he made himself available to them.

BE A LISTENING *PAL*

Quiet Time with Your Child

Presence and availability involve the third element of being a PAL to your children—*listening*. This means that in addition to scheduled time and unscheduled time, there must also be *quiet time*. There are periods when we parents just need to shut our mouths, open our ears, eyes and hearts, and let our children do the talking. In fact, presence and availability don't mean much if a parent isn't listening to his or her kids.

Ben, our middle son, approached me one morning as I was reading the paper. He had something to tell me. "Okay, Son, I'm listening," I said. "What is it you want to tell me?"

He mumbled some words, but because my nose was still in the newspaper, I couldn't quite understand what he was trying to say. Finally, totally exasperated, he crashed through the paper and said, "I want to see your eyes, Dad!"

I had said I was listening. But Ben knew I was only *hearing*. This is a major parental disability: hearing but not listening.

Hidden Messages

Your daughter slams down her math book and says, "I hate math! I don't think this will ever do anybody any good, and furthermore I hate my teacher and my teacher hates me!" What's the message she's trying to get across? Most of us might answer: She hates math and doesn't like her teacher. But what your daughter may be trying to say is, "I don't understand this math, and I'm too far behind and too embarrassed to ask for help. I'm afraid I'm going to fail!"

It sometimes seems our children are speaking in ancient Sanskrit or some secret code, when, in reality, the problem is with us and our failure to listen—I mean truly listen.

There are other scenarios almost all parents have experienced. Your teenager rolls his eyes whenever you speak. Your daughter fidgets, looking for an escape route when you're trying to talk to her. Your son bolts from the room before you can get a word out. For these and many other behaviors, many parents feel estranged from their children. If "women are from Venus and men are from Mars" (as author John Gray argued), sometimes it seems our children are from another galaxy! They may as well be little green beings with antennae for ears.

This attitude causes a parent to shrink away and withdraw on the one hand or to be emotionally and even physically abusive on the other. Such parents lapse into the worldview of W. C. Fields, who said, "The person who hates dogs and children can't be all bad."

Rather than being overwhelmed with the apparent inability to get through, parents must intensify efforts to understand. And that means actually listening to what children are saying behind the codes and murmurings.

HALF CHILD, HALF ADULT

Adolescence means "half child" and "half adult." Young people crawling through this dangerous passage often seem to pull away from their parents. There are two reasons. First, the teenager is awakening to a desire for his or her own identity. It's during these years that children understand their identity has been defined entirely by their family. Now they want to be their "own person." Since the parents represent the family, and the teenager wants to pull away from an identity determined entirely by the family unit, the adolescent child will pull away from the parents. It's part of growing up. The good news is that if parents approach this stage with understanding and skill, their child will ultimately return to the family as the fundamental point of identification and belonging.

The second reason adolescents sometimes pull away from their parents is that mother and father represent childhood to the young person. As they seek to move into their own identity, teens also are attempting to move forward into adulthood. To borrow the Genesis phrase, teenagers are "leaving and cleaving" (see Genesis 2:24 KJV). They are leaving childhood behind with the parents as its prime symbol and "cleaving" to the independence and identity they see as "adulthood."

So we as parents shouldn't make more out of all the eye-rolling, door-slamming, room-bolting than there really is. Certainly it hurts when our kids no longer want to run and jump in our laps or kiss us good-bye on the way to school. But we must not take it personally. Our children are growing up and going through the painful process of discovering life outside the tight bond of a family circle. It is vital in this period for parents to listen and hear. Sometimes the "hearing" is not through an audible form but through the visual communication of body language and facial expressions. It's at this point, too, that parents need to find ways to continue to be involved in their children's lives without crowding them.

WHEN A CHILD SHUTS DOWN

When Jose turned seventeen, his father, Ernesto, could recognize the signs of growing gang involvement on the part of his son. As a child, Jose and his parents and sister were a tight unit. Open lines of communication meant there was healthy interaction in the family. But, at seventeen, Jose was shutting down.

One Friday night Jose was not in at his curfew time, so Ernesto went to search for his son. Ernesto had made it his business to know the community in which his children were growing up. He knew all the gang hangouts. At midnight he found his son sitting on a garbage can in an alley with other young men whose dress and haircuts clearly identified them as gang members.

Ernesto knew he could no longer use disciplinary methods that had been effective when Jose was a child. Instead he determined to find a way to be involved in his boy's life yet let him develop as an adult. Because he understood his son, Ernesto knew a big reason Jose was interested in the gang was because of his fascination with firearms. Ernesto realized he must somehow turn this highly dangerous situation into something positive.

Ernesto never had been interested in guns and never had owned one. Now he decided to buy a rifle and learn to shoot it. On his next birthday, Jose was surprised to discover his dad had bought him a rifle, too. Ernesto and Jose began going to a shooting range where, together, they learned how to use the guns. Eventually, Ernesto and Jose became hunting pals. They spent so many Friday nights and Saturdays camping and hunting, Jose had no time for the gang. Ernesto had sought to understand his son and work with the teenager's interests to deepen their relationship.

This dad understood the importance of time. He worked long hours and often would have preferred a quiet Friday evening and lazy Saturday to sleeping in a tent and hiking through thickets. But Ernesto knew he could tell his son how much he loved him until his teeth fell out, but if he gave Jose none or little of his time, it would only increase the boy's frustration and anger. Kids know the father and mother who say they love them will give their time.

THE FATHER'S FOREVER-FOCUS

Earlier, we talked about David's disastrous offspring. Solomon was an exception—at least for part of his life. When

Solomon dedicated the temple he had built, God spoke to him audibly and unmistakably. "My name [will be] there forever, and My eyes and My heart will be there perpetually," said God (1 Kings 9:3). The Lord was referring to the ark of the covenant, the box made by Moses according to God's command and specifications. The ark represented the literal presence of God. But in A.D. 70 the temple was destroyed and the ark lost. Yet God's promise remains. How, today, can *we* have the Father's name, eyes, and heart forever?

Under the era of the new covenant brought in by Jesus, when we receive Christ as Savior, our bodies become the temple of the Holy Spirit (1 Corinthians 6:19). Jesus Christ dwells within us, the Holy Spirit empowers us, and the promise given to and through Solomon continues in our lives.

As God has done for us, we must do for our children. We give them our name, eyes, and hearts. And we become their PAL because we are *present* at scheduled times, *available* at unscheduled times, and *listening* at quiet times.

Years ago columnist Abigail van Buren of "Dear Abby" fame posed this question to her readers: "If you had it to do over again, would you have children?" Ten thousand people responded. Of those, seven of every ten answered no. That's 70 percent saying they would not have children if they had life to do all over again! There were two primary reasons given: Children are too much responsibility, and they take too much time away from a parent's personal freedom.

The response reflected the contemporary cultural emphasis on self-love as the highest priority for individuals today. Parents learn, however, that self-love must have its place but cannot be the total focus in raising a family. True love, as we noted in a previous chapter, is sacrificial. And for parents, that means giving our time to our children.

QUESTIONS FOR PARENTS

1. If you spent as much time on your business as you do with your children, would your business be a success or failure?

2. Do you control time or does time control you?

3. Have you built into your schedule time for spontaneous "serendipity" activities with your children?

4. What opportunities do your children have for you to be a "spectator," watching them display talents and abilities?

A PERSONAL WORD
Thou Shalt Discipline Thy Children

Here's the chapter many of you have been waiting for. It's the longest chapter in the book. It seems this is the area of parenting that we are most unsure of and generates the most questions. Don't worry, the Bible is clear: If we love our children, we will discipline them.

This chapter will help you discern the difference between discipline and punishment and give you practical advice on positive and healthy discipline for your child.

—E. Y.

Commandment 6

THOU SHALT DISCIPLINE THY CHILDREN

Dads and moms have a supernatural assignment: *They are to be parents, not peers of their kids.* Childhood peers indulge one another and reinforce behaviors, wrong or right. In contrast, parents provide one of the greatest gifts a child will ever receive—discipline.

In May of 2003, America was shocked by a videotaped hazing melee in suburban Chicago. The scenes of teenage girls battering other teenage girls with animal entrails, excrement, and solid objects were chilling. The videotape flashed again and again showing teens lifting up bottles, cans, and cups of beer as the hazing intensified in violence and cruelty. The beer for the underage kids apparently had been supplied by the parents.

"The issue has struck a nerve," said Liza Porteus on a Fox-TV newscast, "among those who believe many parents may be more worried about being a buddy than a father or mother to their teens—to the detriment of both the kids' development and the strength of the family."[1]

THE "WHO" OF DISCIPLINE

Ms. Porteus reported on an ad campaign by Partnership for a Drug-Free America, urging parents to act like adults. "We advise parents that kids have friends; they need parents," said Howard Simon, an executive with the Partnership. "It's important for parents to remember their kids, whether they admit it or not, are looking for you to set rules and boundaries. . . . It's probably the single most important job you have in your life."

And that requires that parents be disciplinarians. As Howard Simon noted, "Your kids need you to give them the rules on how to guide their behavior."[2]

When I was in college, I served as a church youth director. One night I was notified that a teenager in our church had attempted suicide. A policeman asked me to accompany an officer to the house and retrieve the suicide note. When I returned to the hospital emergency room, the parents were wringing their hands, repeating a morbid mantra: "We've done our best. Where did we go wrong? We've done our best. Where did we go wrong?"

Parents have been lifting this lament for generations. You can trace the problem far back through the Old Testament where we find the sad story of Eli and his sons, Hophni and Phinehas. Eli was a God-fearing priest, but his boys feared nothing but missing a "good time." The Bible describes them as "worthless men [who] did not know the Lord" (1 Samuel 2:12). The Hebrew word translated "worthless" means, literally, "sons of Belial." In modern lingo, the term might be rendered "hell raisers." While those words often are regarded as unacceptable slang in polite conversation, they are highly descriptive. They convey the idea of bringing up the dregs and filth from the bubbling slime-pit of hell onto the level of routine human conduct.

The Bible tells it this way:

Now Eli was very old; and he heard all that his sons were doing to all Israel, and how they lay with the women who served
at the doorway of the tent of meeting. He said to them, "Why
do you do such things, the evil things that I hear from all these
people? No, my sons; for the report is not good which I hear
the Lord's people circulating. If one man sins against another,
God will mediate for him; but if a man sins against the Lord,
who can intercede for him?" But they would not listen to the
voice of their father. (1 Samuel 2:22–25)

Eli knew what was up with his sons. He understood they
were guilty of blasphemy, lack of reverence for God, and sexual immorality. Eli was sick with the knowledge that his boys
were hell-raisers. And hell is what they got. The brothers
"brought a curse on themselves," says 1 Samuel 3:13. Eli and
his "house" came under judgment, says 1 Samuel 3:12, because he did not discipline his sons. Eli knew what was up but,
like many parents, walked in denial and self-induced blind-
ness. He didn't have to ask, "Where did I go wrong?" Eli knew
what his sons were doing and took no action to discipline
and correct them.

Eli may have had the hope held by some parents that someone else will get their children under control. But it doesn't
work that way. Those who love, care, and have the highest
level of vision for a child should administer discipline to that
youngster. In most homes, the "who" of discipline is the parent. Discipline fits the parents' calling, responsibility, and job
description.

"OWNERSHIP" MEANS RESPONSIBILITY

Walter loves the water and boats. He was just a young man
when he bought his first craft. His focus was simply getting
on the water and having fun. "I was shocked and surprised
when I became a boat owner to realize I had assumed certain responsibilities along with ownership," he said years

later. Among those responsibilities was the maintenance of the boat and its motor. Walter had to make sure oil was changed, spouts unclogged, gasoline lines properly hooked, and bilges working.

The same is true for a parent. Moms and dads discover that having children is a "package deal." There are plenty of joyful experiences that come with being a parent, but there's also the responsibility of "maintenance," and that includes discipline.

To care properly for our children we must know the difference between discipline and punishment. In this book, I'll use the terms interchangeably, yet there are some important distinctions to note, as shown in "Discipline Versus Punishment" below.

DISCIPLINE VERSUS PUNISHMENT

DISCIPLINE	PUNISHMENT
Sets boundaries for child to grow within	Imposes the penalty for crossing the boundaries
Provides guidance toward goals	Links cause and effect, sowing and reaping, actions and consequences
Holds a person on target toward a purpose	Lays on the price for straying off course
Provides framework for freedom	Provides framework for limitations on liberty when freedom is abused
Proactive behavior of the person in authority toward the individual under authority to help the person achieve his or her best	Reactive behavior of the person in authority toward the one under authority to protect the individual from harm or missing that which is best

When parents confuse discipline and punishment, they assume all discipline is negative and try to steer away from it. Discipline is the "essential positive," and punishment is the sometimes "necessary negative." A developing child will need the balance of both.

Consider again Hophni and Phinehas. They were young men of opportunity. Their father, after all, was the high priest. Eli, in the structure of the nation, was right up there with the king. Had Eli provided discipline for his sons, he might have guided them into magnificent, fruitful destinies. Without the discipline, the boys walked into a grimly inevitable destiny of punishment.

DISCIPLINING STYLES AMONG PARENTS

The Autocratic Parent

There are several parental disciplinary styles.[3] The *autocratic parent* is a dictator in the home. "It's my way or the highway," assert such parents, in no uncertain terms. Repeatedly, children hear from autocratic fathers and mothers, "You'll do it my way or else," or "Don't ask why! Because I said so!" Autocratic parents are strong in punishment-threatening discipline but weak in relationships. They are high on demand and low on responsiveness.

George Brackman, a family counselor, says autocratic parents issue ultimatums to their children such as, "Do this or else!" "There is no discussion or respect for the child's position or request . . . no room for compromise," Dr. Brackman writes. Autocratic parents "give orders and expect immediate obedience—no questions asked."[4]

Autocratic parents tend to develop children who resent authority and are limited in self-expression. Teenagers living with autocratic parents often become rebellious. Frustration develops as the child becomes older and the autocratic styles no longer work. But because communication lines have not been established between the autocratic parent and his or her child, there's only silence—often pained and angry.

The Permissive Parent

The *permissive parent* prides himself or herself in building relationships but is weak in providing the discipline that guides, establishes necessary boundaries, and develops security in the child. A permissive mother might say, "I love my kids so much I can't bring myself to punish them." She has made two mistakes. First, she is confusing punishment and discipline, and, second, she believes punishment and love are opposites.

In addition to being nonpunitive, there are several other characteristics of permissive parents. They really don't want to be in control but would prefer their children to regulate their own behavior. Reason will prevail over power in the attitude of a permissive parent. Children won't have many—if any—household responsibilities if they have permissive parents. They will develop as impulsive people, and are shocked later in life when they discover their bosses won't always consult them on every policy decision.

In fact, according to one study, children of permissive parents "are more likely to be involved in problem behavior and perform less well in school."[5] They will, however, have "higher self-esteem, better social skills, and lower levels of depression."[6]

Many permissive parents were brought up in permissive homes. They were taught they could do anything they wanted, and that's the message they convey to their children. Their kids develop the same skills likely honed in the parents, including manipulation and the utilization of people to gain what they want.

In the purest sense, permissive parents don't love their children. If they did, they would pay the price and make the sacrifices necessary for providing discipline. Love is not the opposite of discipline.

The Indifferent Parent

Love is the opposite of the third parenting style, the *indifferent parent*. This mother or father is weak on both discipline and relationship building. What the child hears from such a parent is, "I don't care." Such parents range from being uninvolved with their children to outright neglect. They minimize interaction with their kids. Children of indifferent parents grow up to be excessively demanding. They lack self-control and refuse to comply with even reasonable standards and rules. They also exhibit aggression.

When Jason was an adult, he looked back on a childhood he regarded as carefree and unobstructed, and realized it was not the lark he thought it was. Every Saturday, his parents would start drinking and continue throughout the weekend. By Sunday, all they could do was sleep all day.

This pattern began when Jason was barely five years old. As a grown man, he understood the danger of a small child left untended. Jason's parents occasionally told him they loved him, but he grew up with the sense that his parents were indifferent. Late in life, Jason's mother and father became serious followers of Jesus Christ and asked their son's forgiveness. But the route to adulthood was rocky for Jason, who had to overcome his own bouts with alcohol, job losses, and marital failures.

The Relational Parent

At the other end of the spectrum from Jason's parents is the *relational parent*. Moms and dads who build relationships have a good understanding of their children through time spent with them. They know the distinct boundaries each child needs.

Relational parents care enough to discipline their kids. These parents understand the vital disciplinary truth that *rules without relationship produce rebellion*. Verbally expressing love without giving time leads to anger. Many children are rebellious and angry because they're brought up by parents who are nonrelational.

Earlier, we considered autocratic parents. Relational parents are *authoritative* without being autocratic. They have the balance of being demanding *and* responsive. University of California researcher Diane Baumrind discovered that such parents utilize disciplinary methods that are primarily supportive rather than merely punitive.[7] Relational, authoritative parents exert control over their children, but because they understand their kids, they build in flexibility. They place limits but foster independence. Boundaries define the "field of play," the "arena of activity," rather than being imprisoning fences. Relational parents make demands on their children, but they explain the reasons the demands are made. Such parents allow for dialogue, for the child to be able to express his or her opinion.

The person developed by such parents knows how to function as part of a team. The child develops confidence in himself or herself and grows in self-reliance and responsibility. Rather than being restless and developing as adults always in search of "greener pastures," whether in marriage or work, people raised by relational, authoritative parents tend to be people of contentment.

There are volumes of research and libraries of "how to" books on parenting. But if we want to become parents who relate to our children properly, exert authority but not tyranny, and discipline effectively, then we will need supernatural wisdom, insight, and love. Our relationship with God will determine the quality of our relationship with our children.

THE "WHERE" OF DISCIPLINE

Where discipline takes place is as important as who administers it. When we discipline our children, we should do so *in private,* not *in public.* In our relationship with the heavenly Father, we know that most of the time He brings discipline to us in deeply personal ways. People in a healthy relationship with God know He's not out to humiliate them. True, when we are in danger, He will sometimes correct us in a way all can see. But this is no different from a loving mother screaming at her child as he darts toward the street. Most often, God speaks to us in that "still, small voice," even when bringing us into discipline.

A parent should never give a harsh reprimand or punishment in front of other people. In one case at least, it was the parent who was humiliated. In September 2002, Madelyne Gorman Toogood was denied a refund from a store in an Indiana shopping center. Already irritated, Toogood's frustration was perhaps fueled by the crying of her small daughter. She returned her four-year-old to the backseat of the car, and then reached inside and began slapping the child and pulling the four-year-old's hair, as the parking lot's videotape cranked away. Toogood ultimately turned herself in to authorities and said her actions recorded on the tape were "pretty much indescribable."[8]

They needed no description, however, because Toogood's actions were played and replayed on television screens across America.

Taking Time to Calm Down and Consider

Thoughtful parents will take their children to a private place to discipline them. This gives parents an opportunity to calm down, cool off, and consider things before they punish. Anytime I punished my boys in anger, the severity of punishment was out of proportion to the offense. I would make absurd, absolutist, and unreasonable pronouncements like, "You'll never drive the car again!" or, "I'm going to send you to school so far away we won't see you until you graduate!" It's important for parents about to punish a child to back up, wait, cool off, and never discipline when angry.

There is an appropriate place to give punishment, and there's a proper place to raise a child. Here in Texas, even in the twenty-first century, there are still vast cattle ranches operated by genuine cowboys and cowgirls. City slickers might think the best place to raise cattle is in a corral where the animals can be watered and fed easily. But the corral is not the best place to raise cattle, because it's too restrictive and confining. Others might figure it to be out on the open range, without fences. But that's not ideal for the raising of cattle either, because the steers will wander off, get mired in bogs, fall into ravines, and be easy targets for predators.

Fenced Pastures Are Best

The best place to raise cattle is in a large pasture bordered by a fence. This is the best of bovine worlds. The cattle have room to wander, but there are boundaries to keep them from meandering into harm's way. And the cattle are clustered close enough that the rancher can count and keep track of them.

An autocratic parent says, "Put those little 'dogies' in the corral where I can keep a close eye on them and run their lives every day." But the kids have no room to grow and develop.

The permissive and indifferent parents declare, "Just let the little 'beasts' run out there on the open range." Sadly, the children get trapped in life's bogs or, worse, are gobbled up by the predators.

John Derbyshire, an English journalist, writes of the problem of "the Life!" He quotes from Tom Wolfe's novel *The Bonfire of the Vanities,* describing a street punk charged with robbery accompanied by three friends to his hearing in a New

York City criminal court. When he sees his friends, the street punk says, "Outta here . . . back to the Life!"

"The Life!" was out in the wide, fenceless land of wandering, the twenty-first-century equivalent of Cain's terrifying Land of Nod (see Genesis 4). Derbyshire interprets "the Life!" as follows:

> Pop music and cool movies . . . current slang and clothing fashions . . . staying up late and going to parties, interacting with the opposite sex, doing things your parents told you not to do, doing things that are slightly illegal, improper or dangerous. . . . For a certain kind of person, the Life! exerts an irresistible gravitational pull. It probably exerts *some* pull on any healthy teenager.[9]

Derbyshire is right. Every generation has had its version of "the Life!" But his concern is the "bohemianization of our culture." In previous eras, there were always moral standards and social limitations, but now all the fences are down, and the broad range where "the Life!" is experienced is a dangerous place.

The best place to raise a kid (no pun intended) is in a pasture. It needs to be broad enough for some serious, curiosity-satisfying grazing. But that pasture needs to be fenced well, along carefully laid boundaries. As the children grow, parents will have to extend the fences. The children will need ever-increasing room for the freedom to make decisions and accept responsibility. Wise parents expand the range where their offspring can develop, and know when to let the fences down altogether. The "where" of discipline, then, is the well-fenced pasture.

THE "WHY" OF DISCIPLINE

The "why" of discipline is given in Hebrews 12:5–7, which says God's children are not to take His discipline lightly, because "those whom the Lord loves He disciplines, and He scourges every son whom He receives. It is for discipline that you endure; God deals with you as with sons; for what son is there whom his father does not discipline?"

The Hebrews passage tells us God disciplines us because He loves us. When we discipline our children, we are signaling our love for them. The child of the indifferent parent has no sense of value or self-worth. It appears the mother or father simply doesn't care enough to correct him, or bring him back to the right path when he's strayed. Discipline is hard, exacting, demanding work, and when we discipline a child, we let him know we care enough to do the job.

Hebrews 12:7 gives us another reason God disciplines us. In doing so, He reaffirms we are part of His family. The heavenly Father's discipline in your life is one of the ways you know you are a born-again, Spirit-energized child of God. When we discipline our children, the unspoken message is, "You are in the family, within the circle of my love and concern. You are high priority to me."

A third reason for discipline is in Hebrews 12:9, which says that "we had earthly fathers to discipline us, and we respected them; shall we not much rather be subject to the Father of spirits and live?" Discipline builds respect. An essential for enjoying a full, productive life is honoring parents (see Exodus 20:12). That's the responsibility of children. Yet mothers and fathers have a responsibility to nurture that honor. Our children may never respect nor honor us if we don't provide them healthy, firm, positive discipline.

Hebrews 12:10 points out that our earthly parents "disciplined us for a short time as seemed best to them, but [God] disciplines us for our good, so that we may share His holiness." God disciplines us for our good, and human fathers and mothers must do the same for their children for the same reason. Discipline builds character and holiness in a person's life. This is why discipline is not a negative but a positive. Proper discipline edifies, builds up.

In Hebrews 12:11 there is a fifth reason God disciplines His children. "All discipline for the moment seems not to be joyful, but sorrowful," says the Scripture, "yet to those who have been trained by it, afterwards it yields the peaceful fruit of righteousness." Discipline is life transforming. The fruit of righteousness is that rich, flavorful, nutritious lifestyle that is vital and alive in the deepest sense. Every parent should want such a life for his or her child, and discipline is essential for attaining it.

THE "HOW" OF DISCIPLINE

So how do we discipline our children? What are the forms, methods, and techniques? Volumes have been written on the subject, but let's consider some of the basics.

Verbal Discipline

First, there is *verbal discipline.* My mother specialized in this disciplinary form. Many a time I would have preferred my father's belt to my mother's correcting words. Disciplinary words are effective tools in a parent's arsenal of discipline.

There must be some guidelines, however. Parents should avoid what the politicians call *ad hominem* attacks. This is an assault on the very core of a person's being and identity. It's one thing to use words to point out the wrongness of a behavior but quite another to tell a child he is useless, stupid, or evil. This is what Jesus had in mind when He spoke of the danger of calling a person a "fool" (Matthew 5:22) in the sense we denigrate and assault the person's personality rather than discipline their actions.

Verbal discipline must operate by a strict economy. If we repeat the same formulas or cliches again and again, our words become meaningless. Verbal discipline must be sharp, targeted, and penetrating. Words become blunted when hurled at the same unyielding target too often.

Grounding Discipline

Grounding is a second form of discipline. Restrictions are placed on special activities. Sending a child to his or her room for a specified period of time is another facet of grounding. It may also include depriving the child of some favored object. "Time-out" is a shortened version of grounding in which the parent requires the child to cool down and restrict his activities so he can give due consideration to the behavior that prompted the discipline.

"Hands-Off" Discipline

"Hands-off" discipline is another form. The operational dynamic for this disciplinary method is the biblical principle of sowing and reaping. After exhaustive efforts to encourage, point out, advise, scold, reprimand, punish, and coerce, there comes a point at which you must remove your protective hand and let the child reap what he has sown.

This principle is detailed in Romans 1. God's wrath "is revealed from heaven against all ungodliness and unrighteousness of men, who suppress truth in unrighteousness," says verse 18. But note the point at which God's wrath is manifest: only *after* people have had so much revelation of His truth and warnings of the consequences of disobedience that they "suppress truth" to carry out their rebellion. Verses 19–20 go on to explain that God has gone to great lengths to show humanity how to live and behave.

Because of continual rejection of God's attempts to lead people into constructive lifestyles, He finally gives them over to their evil desires and their consequences by removing His protective hand (see v. 24).

The "hands-off" method is like learning to ride a bike. When you remove the training wheels, the child will fall off a few times, but usually he will jump right back on and keep trying, with your help, until he learns how to balance the bicycle. Then comes the victorious moment when all the elements of bike riding come together, and your child zips off down the street all by himself. Watching the exhilaration of achievement on your child's face is worth the scary sight of all the falls.

WHEN TO INTERVENE

Several years ago Jo Beth and I were at a picnic with one of our sons. He was just a few years old and, like all curious kids, kept wandering off. Each time, Jo Beth or I would bring him back and talk to him about the dangers of roaming off. He learned nothing from our lectures, however, and kept walking away.

At one point, Jo Beth looked at me and said, "Would you believe it? He's running off again, and this time he's going into the woods!"

The "Hands-Off" Approach in Action

"Just let him go this time," I said, keeping an eye on my son to make sure he didn't get too far away.

I watched from a distance as he meandered down a path, picking up a stick here, inspecting a leaf there. He could still see us and felt the security of that visual link. However, he finally disappeared from view. As soon as he lost sight of Jo Beth and me, he began to whimper. Quickly, I moved to a position where I could see him but he couldn't spot me. He wandered this way and that, running, then walking. Slowly his dilemma dawned on him.

"I'm lost!" he cried.

It was time to intervene.

I scampered up to him and picked him up. "That's what happens when you wander off," I said to him.

Several years later, another of our sons wasn't doing well in a certain class, largely because he wasn't taking it seriously. Repeatedly, I warned him that if he didn't start studying and doing his homework, he would be academically ineligible to play basketball. "That'll never happen to me, Dad," he would respond. Unfortunately, it did. When he had to sit out two crucial games because of his poor grades in the class, he learned the valuable lesson. "Hands-off" discipline is hard on the parent, because we all want to protect our children and see them succeed.

The "Hands-On" Approach

But *"hands-on"* discipline, a fourth kind of discipline, is even harder. Of course it's not usually your hands you're using. Most parents use a wooden spoon, paddle, or belt. This form of discipline must be appropriate to the situation, age, and gender. Parents must also understand the proper use of the "rod."

Biblical "spanking" is understood in the context of Proverbs 22:6, "Train up a child in the way he should go, [and] even when he is old he will not depart from it." The Hebrew word for "train" in the original text means to "narrow" something. The imagery is that of a shepherd leading his sheep across a broad field. He must keep them on a specific path, lest they wander off into danger. So he uses a rod, not to thrash the sheep, but to prod and coax them back to the defined, narrow path that takes them directly to the sheepfold, water, or grass.

So, with the picture of the shepherd coaxing his sheep along the way in mind, Proverbs 13:24 says, "He who spares his rod hates his son, but he who loves him disciplines him diligently." A shepherd who wouldn't use his rod to guide wandering sheep back to the path would be fired. It would demonstrate the shepherd had no care for the sheep. The parent who cares for his children will discipline them "diligently." The writer of Proverbs is talking here of corrective discipline.

GUIDELINES FOR SPANKING

An Option to Consider

It is the worst of shepherds and parents who use the rod to thrash and wound. In doing so, parents actually can bring physical and mental harm to the child. However, properly administered, the gentle, "coaxing" use of the rod can be effective and should be an option.

In a recent study at the University of California at Berkeley, research psychologists Diana Baumrind and Elizabeth Owens found that "occasional spanking does not damage a child's social or emotional development."[10] Baumrind concluded, "What really matters is the child-rearing context. When parents are loving and firm and communicate well with the child, the children are exceptionally competent and well adjusted, whether or not their parents spanked them as preschoolers."[11] This type of discipline, she suggested, is best exercised by authoritative parents.

Baumrind has also provided guidelines for "appropriate" spanking, as follows:

- Spanking must be controlled.
- Spanking should be contingent on the child's behavior.
- Spanking should be administered only after the child is forewarned.
- Spanking should be given under conditions when the parent uses more positive than negative incentives.
- Spanking should immediately follow the behavior to be corrected.
- Spanking must be rendered by a calm parent.

- Spanking should be done privately.
- Spanking ought to be carried out in conjunction with reasoning.
- Spanking must have the intention to correct, not to retaliate.
- Spanking must be mild and not escalate to abuse.
- Spanking ought not be given children under eighteen months or past puberty.[12]

I would add that spanking ought to be the last resort, not the first.

These guidelines reflect the biblical intent of spanking. Many parents, for example, make a mistake by not being sensitive to the age of a child when they spank. Dr. Baumrind says a baby under eighteen months should not be spanked. Yet the first response of some mothers and fathers is to whack the tyke as he heads for the electrical plug. Children at this stage are explorers, and they probe things with their touch. Spanking at this age sends the wrong message. The most effective form of discipline at the pre-eighteen-month stage is a stern verbal warning.

Consistent and Specific

By the way, "consistency" is the most important word in discipline. That's the way a child makes the mental connection between the parents' words and tone, and behaviors that are to be avoided.

Spanking, we noted, must be situation-, age-, and gender-appropriate. However, all discipline should be customized. There is no "one size fits all" disciplinary methodology. My son Ed's brain seemed not to register our corrective messages until his posterior felt the biting—but not brutal—sting of my belt. Ben responded to straight, strong logic. All we had to do with Cliff was give him a stern look or word. If I had used a cookie cutter approach by employing the same form of discipline for all our boys, ignoring their personalities, I would have been ineffective and perhaps damaged them.

Kids sometimes don't believe parents who say, "This hurts me more than you." But I must confess that I cried along with my boys every time I spanked them.

HELP THE CHILD UNDERSTAND "WHY"

It's important, too, that the child understand why he—and you—are having to experience the pain of discipline. Explain to your little one the reason for the punishment. Help him make the link between behaviors and consequences.

After the explanation and spanking comes repentance and forgiveness. Just as the child must connect actions and outcomes, he must be able to link repentance with forgiveness. It's helpful to teach the child the meaning of repentance as "turning around" and moving in a new, better direction. Lead the child in acknowledging repentance and asking forgiveness of God and any other person affected by the wrong behavior. Then help the child receive forgiveness. Show your child that what God forgives He forgets and removes from us, so there is no need for him to continue to walk in guilt. Give plenty of hugs.

Discipline and punishment are great opportunities to teach children the nature of unconditional love. As they see you love them no matter what, they grow with a healthy attitude toward themselves and others. They grasp the fact that people make mistakes, but, because of Jesus Christ and His grace, there can always be a new beginning. This is the distinctive dimension that biblical truth brings to the entire matter of discipline, and why discipline is an important tool in helping your child develop spiritually as well as emotionally and mentally.

THE "WHAT" OF DISCIPLINE

Now comes the final question: *What do we discipline?*

Dealing with the Small Stuff

Two principles guide us in answering this question. First, *don't sweat the small stuff.* Imagine you drive home in a minefield of traffic after a day on the battlefield of work. You have a throbbing headache worsened by the sound of metal bending and cracking. Your dear child has left his bicycle on the driveway, despite your many warnings. You get out, move the bike wreckage and ease into the garage, only to discover two fishing poles lying on the floor where you park your car. You back out the auto, move the rods, pull back in, and park. Now you discover the back door ajar and the entire neighborhood being air-conditioned, courtesy of your son. Once in the house, you hear the TV set blaring, even though you issued an edict that no one watches television at this hour on a weeknight. You walk into the den, and there he sits in front of the screen. He looks up with a million-dollar smile and says, "How's it going, Dad?"

What do you do? Grrrrrrrrrrrrrrrrrr! But it's at precisely this point you have to stop and ask yourself: *Is this worth tearing into my son?* Probably not. It's irritating, yes, but these infractions could hardly be classified as family felonies.

The better approach to take in that situation might be to begin a conversation with your son that turns him away from the TV. Then you might say something like, "I'm so stressed out I need to walk around the block. Come with me." That's the time to discuss coolly and calmly what you found when you got home and to go over the rules about bicycles, fishing rod storage, and television schedules one more time.

Dealing with the Big Stuff

All this makes you much more credible when you have to deal with the big stuff. That brings us to the second principle to consider as you contemplate what to discipline: *Deal skill-fully and proportionately with the major issues.*

The "big stuff" consists of three areas. First is *morality*. Children must be taught the difference between right and wrong. The second "big stuff" category is *ethics*. This is the behavioral application of a moral lifestyle. Third, "big stuff" deals with the *physical consequences* of a child's actions. These are the three points on the battleground where you draw the clear, concise, unmistakable lines and haul out the heavy artillery. Examples include drugs and alcohol, sexual promiscuity, profanity, lack of respect for others and their property, lying, cheating, and stealing.

The United States is the world's "superpower." But the military strategists don't hurl a nuclear missile at every problem. There are miscreant nations whose threats are met by small "police actions." There are larger challenges (such as Iraq) that call for sweeping conventional invasion and "regime change." Hovering over humanity is the sinister shadow of nuclear nations for whom America may have to reserve her own atomic warheads.

In a fallen world, there will always be a "superpower." Thank God it's a nation like America, which has no desire for empire, whose value system enshrines liberty for all, and which has a thoughtful approach to the use of her power against less powerful but sometimes troubling countries.

In a home in the fallen world, there must also be a "superpower." It must be the parents who understand where, when, why, what, and how they are to discipline their children.

Mothers and fathers who discipline with such comprehensive skill are not just "superpowers" but *super parents!*

QUESTIONS FOR PARENTS

1. What forms of discipline helped you the most when you were a child?

2. What forms of discipline were ineffective in correcting you when you were a child?

3. What's the difference between *punitive* and *corrective* discipline?

4. When it comes to the discipline of your children, do your actions show you are raising them in a narrow "corral," a broad, unbounded "open range," or a fenced "pasture"?

A PERSONAL WORD
Thou Shalt Encourage Thy Children

Get your pom-poms ready, mom and dad. You're about to become a cheerleader! You need to be your child's biggest fan, so read on for ways to cheer your son or your daughter on to successful, secure living. Let's hear it for the Eagles!

—E. Y.

Commandment 7

THOU SHALT ENCOURAGE THY CHILDREN

Encouragement is a vital facet of discipline. Effective parents establish boundaries, not to imprison their children but to set the dimensions of their field of freedom. Successful mothers and fathers then become cheerleaders, rooting for their kids to explore, discover, and take advantage of all the opportunities up to—but not beyond—the boundaries. Healthy children know that inside the boundaries are life, light, and thrilling adventure. But looming outside are death, darkness, and terror.

Many earthbound human beings consider a bird the freest of animals. We watch with envy as the feathery creatures bound upward, zoom downward, and surf on the air. Yet even the birds have boundaries. They fly within the atmosphere. If they tried to exceed the limits of the sky, they would find themselves in a dark, cold vacuum where life would endure barely seconds.

Children and birds were meant to have wonderful zones

for soaring, and to be encouraged to ascend as high as possible without crossing over into darkness and death.

AN EAGLE OR A PRAIRIE CHICKEN?

Once a prairie chicken spotted a lone egg. She sat on it until the egg hatched—out popped a baby eagle. Neither newborn eaglets nor momma prairie chickens are noted for their capacity for self-reflection, so neither understood the eagle was an eagle and not a prairie chicken. The eaglet, therefore, was brought up as a prairie chicken. It waddled according to the only example of walking it had, ate garbage, and stayed on the ground.

One day the baby eagle looked up and saw a majestic creature gliding through the sky. Prairie chicken momma came over and said, "No use lookin' up there at that bird. That's an eagle. You'll never be like that. We're prairie chickens."

So the eagle spent his life looking up wistfully at the sky, longing to skim the clouds. He never understood he was an eagle—that all he had to do was flap his wings and fly.

Are you raising eagles or prairie chickens?

There was a lady in the Bible determined to raise her two boys as eagles. Normally we smirk when we read about Salome, the audacious mother of James and John. She's the one who makes a special request of Jesus. "Command that in Your kingdom these two sons of mine may sit, one on Your right and one on Your left" (Matthew 20:21).

Talk about a pushy mother!

JESUS' RESPONSE

Note, however, Jesus' response. He tells her that "to sit on My right and on My left, this is not Mine to give, but it is for those for whom it has been prepared by My Father" (v. 23). Though one with the Father, Jesus as the Incarnate Son had voluntarily subjected Himself to certain limitations (for ex-

ample, see Philippians 2:5–11). That included the position-
ing of people around the throne of heaven. Further, said Jesus, the greatest in His kingdom are servants.

There's something missing in Jesus' answer to Salome. The
Man who had no problem calling the Pharisees a generation
of snakes and turning over money-changers' tables in the temple, does not rebuke Salome for her seemingly presumptu-
ous request for her sons. I want to say, "Lady, you are arrogant
and out of bounds!" In the contemporary world, Salome
would have been one of those notorious soccer moms or Little League dads demanding that the coach give their gawk-
ing child the key position on the big play.

Actually, it's unfortunate this mother has gotten such a bum
rap. Truth is, she was a special mother. First, she was one of
the women who stayed at the cross when Jesus was nailed to it.
Second, this feisty lady was among the first to get to the tomb
when Jesus arose from the dead (Matthew 27:56; Mark 16:1).

Okay, she may have been too forward in trying to get the
lock on an eternal position for her sons. But isn't that just
like a mother? What's abnormal about a mom wanting the best
for her kids? What's to condemn in that?

Apparently nothing, because Jesus does not condemn Salome for her request but merely clarifies her understanding of
the nature of His kingdom.

AHEAD OF THE CURVE

Salome was ahead of the curve. When she made her request to Jesus, not many recognized Him as Messiah. Most
still saw Him as a wandering preacher and erstwhile carpen-
ter. But Salome saw Jesus as He really was. She knew someday He would have a kingdom greater than all, and the highest
honor would be for her boys to get the best seats in the house.
This lady was way out front of everyone in her understanding of faith, prophecy, and what was really going on.

Salome also teaches us about seeing our kids as VIP material. She was not a prairie chicken, and she had no intention of raising prairie chickens. Salome was in the eagle-producing business. Maybe her sons were embarrassed by their mom's audacity, but down deep inside they had to have been encouraged by her confidence in them. It also gave the boys an opportunity to hear Jesus' important teachings about authority, servanthood, leadership, and, above all, identification with Him.

These were the very principles James and John put into practice in their lives. James was the first of the apostles to die as a martyr. John is paired with Paul as one of the two most important people in the New Testament, after Jesus. It was John, early in his life, who leaned on Jesus at the Last Supper and held up Mary as she watched her Son die on the cross. It was also John, as an elderly man, who was exiled to Patmos and there recorded the incredible visions we know as the book of Revelation.

James and John turned out to be eagles!

So we shouldn't condemn Salome based on one clip from her history. Rather, we need to observe the fruit of her life and the whole of Scripture in evaluating this mother. Things are not always what they seem. The Bible warns us against judging people based on appearance (2 Corinthians 10:7; James 2). A deeper, longer look at Salome demonstrates the quality woman and mother she really was.

Like all parents, Salome was a mirror in which her sons could see an image of themselves. What they saw was the vision of two young men so excellent their mother figured they deserved sitting at Jesus' right and left. There is obviously the danger of spoiling children with a delusionary view. This happens in a home where there is no discipline and the kids are told only how wonderful they are, not where they need to improve. But the encouraging parent will give continual feedback of the positive, along with the correctional.

There's another way parents are mirrors for their children, and this view may not always be so positive. Our kids look at us and see what they will become when they grow up. One of the ways we encourage our children is by setting in front of them a vision of hope—not dread—that they will be like us.

DEFIANCE OR ASPIRATION?

A young man I'll call Billy was humiliated constantly by his father, an alcoholic. His dad's alcoholism was a matter of public record and comment. Many nights, Billy's terrified mom had to call the police to rescue her and her children from her terrorizing husband. Billy was embarrassed that the neighbors saw the squad car at his house night after night, hauling off his screaming father. "I will never be like my father!" Billy vowed. It was a *commitment to defiance.*

Randall's father set before his son a *positive aspiration.* The dad lived before his family, his work associates, and his community such an exemplary life that Randall would point at his father and say, "That's my dad; I'm going to be like him someday!" Randall looked in the mirror of his father's lifestyle and saw hope, a positive image into which he determined to grow.

Let me point out that parents aren't the only mirrors our children encounter. They live in a society filled with reflecting mirrors. Mark's teachers accused him of being lazy and dumb. So he slogged through life, believing he was indeed lazy and dumb.

Peers made fun of Sally's legs. "You've got bird legs!" they would taunt. Sally never went swimming or wore pretty dresses that might expose her legs.

Chris was quarterback of his football team, leading his school to a district championship. He was acclaimed because he was a winning football player.

Mark, Sally, and Chris, like most children, are on tread-mills of worldly acceptance. Treadmills are dead-end devices, going nowhere. They also can be dangerous. If a treadmill gets stuck suddenly when you're jogging or running, you can get thrown off. I speak from experience. Many people on a tread-mill of apparent success thud to the ground when the applause stops suddenly. They are emotionally and mentally broken. All three of these kids are in trouble. As long as they see them-selves through the lens of other people, they will never view themselves as God does.

We must encourage our children to distinguish among achievement, external appearance, and core identity. Abraham Lincoln was not stymied by his lanky, gawky, gnarled physique. Winston Churchill wasn't held back by his pudgy, chalky, bald appearance. Both these men experienced stag-gering political crashes causing critics to write their profes-sional obituaries. But it was *after* Lincoln and Churchill had been consigned to the political graveyard that they became two of modern history's greatest leaders. Our kids need our encouragement to ignore the external handicaps and not al-low the limitations to determine how high they can fly.

WAYS TO ENCOURAGE YOUR CHILDREN

Encourage Unconditional Love

There are three specific focal points for encouraging chil-dren.

First, *encourage your children to recognize and receive true unconditional love.* To do that, fathers and mothers must grasp the meaning of the highest variety of love. In the world prior to the Bible, people understood love in a way that is described by the Greek words *eros*, referring to romantic love, and *phileo*, the word for friendship love. These two forms of "love" oc-cur because there is something desirable in a person that attracts our attention. A man is attractive and desirable to a woman, and she falls in love with him, or vice versa. An associate shares our likes and dislikes and makes us happy to be around, and we cultivate a friendship.

Jesus showed the world something it had never before seen, a style of love the Greek language called *agape* (a-gop-ay). *Eros* and *phileo* happen because a person gets fulfillment and satisfaction from another, either through a romantic involvement or friendship or both. That is, the person loved gives the lover something he or she wants. *Agape* love "is a free and decisive act determined by its subject," notes one linguistic expert.[1]

Parents who love their children unconditionally do so because they have chosen to cherish their kids no matter what the cost or grief—even if the children are unable to return anything of satisfaction to their parents.

No more beautiful modern story of such parental love can be found than that of John and Christine Haggai for their son, Johnny. John Haggai, a noted evangelist, author, and global missions leader, chronicled the story in his book *My Son Johnny*. Johnny Haggai was born November 27, 1950, delivered by a physician whose neglect and mismanagement of the complicated birth resulted in the child's being spastic and con fined to a wheelchair.

Twenty-four years later, as Johnny lay dying, John wrote, "My son has never entered into a normal conversation. He can't talk. He has never played a round of golf. He can't walk. He has never taken anybody out to lunch. He can't feed himself. He has never tied a Windsor knot. He can't dress himself."[2]

Yet from the moment Johnny was born, John and Christine poured their love on the struggling infant. In another place and time, the eugenics proponents would have cast Johnny aside. But Johnny's parents chose from day one to make their son the object of unconditional love. Johnny blossomed under that radiance from his father and mother.

Though Johnny couldn't travel with his father on his worldwide treks, he became his dad's top intercessory partner. He and John worked out a system of communication, and Johnny's uncanny ability to read people made him a strategic advisor to his father.

As John flew home from the South Pacific to be with his son in his last hours, he wrote, "I need him. I can't afford to lose him, but I know that the time has come to give him up."

Johnny Haggai had grown into a powerful man spiritually, emotionally, and mentally—a treasured colaborer with his father in his ministry. His true development began and was continually encouraged by the unconditional love of his parents.

Encourage Awareness of Spiritual Gifts

Second, it's important for parents to encourage their children *to know and happily embrace their spiritual gifts.* John and Christine Haggai helped Johnny understand that he was a gifted person, not a "handicapped" individual.

Spiritual gifts are part of the salvation "package" a person receives when he or she is born again spiritually through Jesus Christ. Imparted by the Holy Spirit directly to the individual, spiritual gifts are the God-given abilities by which a person who has received Jesus Christ is able to do the works of Christ and His kingdom. God determines what spiritual gifts a person will have (see especially 1 Corinthians 12:1–18).

Encourage Appreciation of Personality

The third focal point for encouraging children is to *help each child understand and appreciate his or her personality.* There is a direct link between spiritual gifts and personality type. Human personality is the repository of one's spiritual gifts. Therefore, the personality will be shaped uniquely for the complex of spiritual gifts God chooses to give the individual.

If you visit Windsor Palace in England, you will see suits of armor worn over the centuries by various members of British royalty. It's easy to spot the armor of King Henry VIII. All his portraits depict him as a stocky man, with a sizable "pot belly." So the armor reflects the contours of King Henry's body. In the same way, an individual's personality is designed for the profile of the individual's spiritual gifts.

A person, then, with a gift of administration may not be as outgoing as one with the spiritual gift of hospitality, but the hospitable person may not have the eye for detail as the administrator. The prophet may not have the same upbeat personality as the exhorter or encourager, but the encourager may not be as forthright as the prophet. The mercy-person perhaps will not have the same personality type as the discerner and will need the person with discernment to keep the mercy-giver from falling for every sad scam.

Many people think there is a one-size-fits-all personality type. They try to force themselves into being something they weren't designed to be. It's especially tragic when parents try to force change in their children's core personalities. Such action is opposite of the encouragement that leads to healthy personality development.

As our children grow up, their personalities are developing under the guidance of God's spiritual "DNA" to fit the spiritual gifts He has selected for them, according to His ordained purpose for their lives. It's therefore vital for parents to watch carefully the type of personality developing in their child, and not try to change it but cultivate it. There is an embryonic personality needing nourishment, just as there are embryonic hands, arms, feet, legs, necks, and heads.

"As the twig is bent, the tree inclines," wrote the ancient poet Virgil. This is among the meanings of Proverbs 22:6, which says, "Train up a child in the way he should go, even when he is old he will not depart from it." The phrase "the way he should go" refers to noting the personality tendencies of the child and, through discipline and encouragement, "bending" him or her in the direction indicated by the child's outward expressions.

This means we must be closely observant of the nature of each one of our children and encourage personality development that conforms to the child's God-given nature. We should not try to shape children in our own personality mold but detect the type God has given the child and stimulate the growth of that unique personality.

UNHEALTHY AND HEALTHY SELF-ESTEEM

Unhealthy Self-Esteem

Showing unconditional love and encouraging the giftedness and personality of a child will lead to healthy self-esteem in the youngster. There is much debate over how best to establish self-esteem in children. In fact, a "self-esteem movement" has been launched with an often wrongheaded understanding of what constitutes self-esteem. Self-centeredness is the twisted definition many have embraced for self-esteem. By all human measures, this version of the "self-esteem movement" has been a spectacular success. Yet the numbers, experts agree, are both misleading and giving a false degree of self-esteem to children enrolled in our nation's schools.

Diane Ravitch, professor of education at New York University, after reviewing comments by foreign students who found American schools easier and less demanding on academic subjects, said, "Our students tend to have more self-esteem than is apparently warranted."[3] And, George Mason university professor Walter Williams, in commenting on the decline of American education, wrote:

While American students trail their counterparts in other countries in just about every academic area, they have the highest levels of self-esteem and feel good about their educational achievements. That's sad. They're fools and don't know it.[4]

A collectivistic approach to self-esteem—institutions saying all people are Okay—is impersonal and usually dishonest and unhealthy.

Healthy Self-Esteem: The Task of the Parents

The problem is not with self-esteem but with *who* encourages it, *how* they define it, and *where* self-esteem is encouraged. Healthy self-esteem is developed by parents. If the task of encouraging self-esteem is left to schools, students will be seen as groups more than as individuals.

In fact, the desire by schools to help children "feel good about themselves" may be the cause of such practices as "grade inflation," by which students are given higher grades even though their work may be inferior to others. Glenn Ricketts of the National Association of Scholars identified grade inflation as "part of the general malaise in higher education." Some schools, he said, "don't want to give students the grades they deserve; they're afraid of hurting their feelings."[5]

When parents encourage self-esteem in their own children, they deal with each child as an individual. The father and mother are aware not only of the positive attributes and potentials of their child but also of the obstacles in his make-up that must be overcome to achieve all the possibilities of his sparkling personality. A collectivist approach to self-esteem development will ignore the limitations and obstacles for fear of socio-economic "profiling," or being politically incorrect.

Encouraging healthy self-esteem in a child is the task of parents, not impersonal institutions!

WAYS TO BUILD ESTEEM IN YOUR CHILDREN

The truth is our children will respect themselves largely on the basis of how they see us as parents. When somebody speaks your name, what do you think comes to your child's mind? How do your children see you?

Encourage Them

Some parents are viewed as critics, or possessing negative personalities. Others are seen as playmates. Yet other dads and moms are viewed by their kids as encouragers. If your children were asked, how would they characterize you?

Family counselor and advocate James Dobson says parents should say seven positive things to their children before speaking one negative. Seven positives, seven pats on the back before speaking negatively about a child's actions.

Participate with Them

When I was a boy, my dad and I were pals. He played with me and took me places. He trained and taught me about life. He used the best form of education, teaching me through allowing me to do things with him. He would perform some feat, work out some practical problem, and let me watch him. Then he would allow me to do some of the work, under his guidance. This is the way you encourage and develop kids. You involve them with you, gradually releasing to them more responsibility until they are able to accomplish the task by themselves.

My father followed this approach until I was a teen. Then he became ill, and things began to change. Somewhere along the way he withdrew and I withdrew. The relationship once so vital and alive drifted into distant doldrums. Until his death, I sought to restore the relationship, but he could no longer respond. I knew he would be there if anything went wrong in my life, but he was no longer a direct, interested participant.

I really missed his encouragement. Instead, we then had what I would call a *blah* relationship, because the dynamics had disappeared.

Some parents have a blah relationship with their children, and it's not due to illness. You're there, but you're not there. The kids know they could always count on you if they really needed you, but there's no real relationship, so they do their best to make it without you—you're just on standby alert. You might say, "Well, a *blah* relationship is better than a negative one!" Actually, both hurt. It's essential for parents to be encouragers. Our children will know they can count on us, so they will choose to come to us with their problems, dilemmas, and successes.

Watch What You Say

How do we become encouragers? First, we must watch our speech. "Let no unwholesome word proceed from your mouth," says Ephesians 4:29. "Unwholesome," in the original language, means "rotten" or "spoiled." Think of a dead fish lying in the sun two or three days and you get the picture. The resulting stench is the natural equivalent of unwholesome words to your kids. Unwholesome words run the gamut from profanity to overreacting hyperbole to searing blasts of anger. Instead, says Ephesians 4:15, we are to "speak the truth in love." Speaking the truth means we lay out the hard, disciplinary, correcting facts. But doing it "in love" describes the style of delivery that helps rather than wounds.

Ephesians 4:29 goes on to say that we should utter "only such a word as is good for edification according to the need of the moment, so that it will give grace to those who hear." There are words that tear down, and there is speech that builds up, or edifies. Encouraging parents are those whose kids are enhanced after conversations and encounters with their parents—even those difficult "talks."

In fact, the church itself ought to be a community of encouragement. Mutual edification ought to be a habitual practice. There ought to be a flow within the community of encouragement from church to home to church. That way, people will develop a positive, edifying lifestyle, and children will be in a continuum of encouragement.

There is, for example, an unfortunate technique used by some athletic coaches. A four-foot little guy misses a basket on a ten-foot stanchion, and the coach bellows across the court, "I'm gonna take you out of the game if you don't start hittin' your shots!" The threatening voice ricochets off the hard floor and walls, and everyone giggles at the "basketball-challenged" youngster. This may be ridiculous as a coaching technique, but it's even worse when parents join the dooming chorus.

It's much better to say, "Great try! Keep taking good shots! Don't worry about it! It's going to go in the basket!" I can still remember a great coach I had as a youngster. "Boy, I like the way you hustle," he said to me one day. It made me feel like a brand-new guy. The coach's words gave me a renewed confidence and left me with a satisfaction I can still feel after all these decades. I wasn't the fastest player on the team, but from that point forward, no one out-hustled me!

Affirm . . . Affirm . . . Affirm

A friend in Florida told me of a junior high student who was a troublemaker with a capital *T*. One day the boy's father received yet another call about his son. The principal asked if he could meet with the father. The dad braced for the worst. When he arrived at the school, the father was ushered in to meet the principal, who was accompanied by a teacher the dad had never met.

"I want to tell you about your son," said the teacher. Then he listed ten positive qualities about the boy.

"That's great," said the father. "Now give me the bad news."

The teacher looked at him. "But that's all I have to say," he replied.

When the dad returned home, his son asked what the principal and teacher had to say. The father listed the ten positive statements made about his son. In no more than two weeks there was a transformation in the boy. He changed from being a troublemaker to an outstanding student with excellent conduct. The youngster developed great relationships with his principal, teachers, and fellow students. Encouragement had been like sunshine on seed that had lain dormant a long time, and the boy began to bloom.

Be Honest and Balanced in Your Words

My wife, Jo Beth, excels at spotting those special opportunities to give encouragement. When our son Ed was just a young pastor on our staff, he was assigned the pastoral prayer in our worship service. We had several pastors who shared this responsibility week after week—they would have a prayer and then lead the congregation in reciting the Lord's Prayer. Now anyone who has spoken in front of a crowd understands "momentary amnesia"—those times when we "go blank" or "lose our train of thought." So I encouraged our pastors always to have the Lord's Prayer written out in their Bibles.

Being young and of sound mind, Ed felt he would never forget something as familiar as the Lord's Prayer. So he approached the pulpit at the assigned time in the service and prayed a beautiful prayer. He then proceeded into the Lord's Prayer: "Our Father, which art in heaven, hallowed be Thy name. . . ." At that moment, somewhere in Ed's brain, steel doors slammed shut. He hesitated and then began to fumble around for the right words.

Fortunately, the congregation bailed him out. They kept right on praying, as Ed stood quietly at the microphone. He felt terrible! It really bothered him that he had "messed up."

After the service, Jo Beth was there to encourage our embarrassed son. "Ed, your voice sounded so good today," she said as she patted him on the arm. I'm afraid I wasn't as encouraging. However, Jo Beth gave Ed the "Way to go!" while I administered the corrective word. Such a balance produces eagles rather than prairie chickens.

Accept Them As They Are

Encouraging your children begins by accepting them as they are. Remember, God accepted you when you were not acceptable by the standards of His character. Some people think God is like an emergency room physician who says to a man with a broken arm, "Heal your arm then come back to the hospital." That's not the way it works on the earthly plane or on the heavenly. God takes us broken, battered, bruised, and beaten. "God demonstrates His own love toward us, in that while we were yet sinners, Christ died for us" (Romans 5:8). That means when you and I were at our worst, God gave His best for us.

Jesus modeled that on the practical level. We see it in two encounters He had with adulterous women (John 4 and 8). He didn't scold them and say, "Get your act together!" Though He didn't condone their sin, He gave them unconditional love, grace, forgiveness, and a second chance. That's foundational for encouraging our children.

Share Your '"Bones"

Next, to encourage healthy self-esteem, parents need to care for their children in practical, demonstrable ways kids can experience. This requires an understanding of the anatomy of encouragement and the skeletal framework that holds it together. Fathers and mothers must keep their kids so close that they share their "bones" with them.

First, we can *demonstrate caring by sharing our "wishbones"* with our children. That is, we need to nurture vision in our kids by communicating our dreams and aspirations, and inspiring them to tell us theirs.

Next we *share our "jawbones."* This means taking the time to tell life stories to our children. Every family needs its sagas, its canon of tales and traditions. Like the stones Joshua placed in the middle of the Jordan after Israel's crossing into the Promised Land, these stories become monuments by which our children remember important lessons in living. They can pass the stories on to *their* children one day.

We must also *share the "anklebone."* Simply put, we should walk with our children and allow them to walk with us. Sharing experiences is a vital means of helping our kids feel they are part of our lives, not just sidelined observers.

Finally, we *share our "backbone"* with our children. This has to do with being consistent and balanced in our discipline. We maintain the firmness but in the equilibrium of love and understanding. We know the "when" and "how" of discipline, as we described it in the previous chapter, but we know also when to show grace and mercy.

In his autobiography, *The Ragman's Son,* actor Kirk Douglas recalled being in a high school play. He sang, danced, and had a speaking role. Douglas knew his mother would be present for his performance but not his father. His dad was distant and cold and rarely spoke anything to his son that was not stern and threatening. So he was surprised the night of the play to spot his father seated at the rear of the auditorium.

The young actor was thrilled and hoped his father would give him encouragement. He desperately wanted to hear his dad say, "Well done!" Instead, after the play Kirk Douglas's father stood there like a brick wall.

Suddenly, though, there was a slight change. The dour Russian immigrant asked his son if he would like to go get an ice cream cone. Years later, Douglas said that five-cent ice cream cone meant even more to him than his Oscar.[6]

AN EAGLE WHO BECAME AN EAGLE

Charlotte Morris grew up in a series of broken homes. Five different fathers paraded before her, with four different mothers. Twice, Charlotte was adopted. Tossed from family to family, Charlotte had just crossed the teenage threshold when someone different entered her life. It was a neighbor who was sensitive to the young girl's roller-coaster life —a neighbor who knew the difference between prairie chickens and eagles.

He began to encourage Charlotte daily in everything she did. His encouragement included getting her linked with a church and its youth group.

At age fifteen, Charlotte began supporting herself. When she was seventeen, she moved into an eight-foot-wide house trailer in San Angelo, Texas. The high-school senior somehow balanced her studies with a job tossing hamburgers and french fries.

After graduating, Charlotte moved herself to Houston, where she enrolled in college. Still, there was no one else to support her, and it took Charlotte eleven years to complete her undergraduate degree. However, she excelled in academics and went straight into a masters' degree program, which she finished in two years.

Ultimately, Charlotte became a leader in the Houston branch of a Baptist home for children prior to joining our church staff. All the lives Charlotte has touched with blessing and inspiration indirectly flowed from the encouragement that came from her neighbor when Charlotte was thirteen years old.

Charlotte Morris is an eagle, and she has inspired others to overcome the hefty tug of the gravity of tribulation. If you want your kids to be eagles rather than prairie chickens, give them heaping, constant doses of genuine encouragement to flap their wings and soar!

QUESTIONS FOR PARENTS

1. What attitudes are you cultivating in your children that *limit* their horizons?

2. What steps are you taking to identify your children's potentials and to help them develop toward the realization of those potentials?

3. Who was the greatest encourager in your life, and what was it he or she did that motivated and inspired you?

4. How will you help your child understand and know his or her spiritual gifts?

A PERSONAL WORD
Thou Shalt Provide Stability and Security for Thy Children

Get your hard hats on—we're headed into a construction zone. Parents, no matter what your vocation, you are a construction worker. You're the foreman in charge of building a beautiful temple for the God of this universe! This chapter has the necessary blueprints for making sure the temple—your child—is stable and secure.

—E. Y.

Commandment 8

THOU SHALT PROVIDE STABILITY AND SECURITY FOR THY CHILDREN

Parents are not only raising children, they're building temples. That's right. Since human beings are made to be filled with God's presence, parents are temple builders, laying a solid foundation of discipline covered by a sturdy roof of encouragement. Connecting the foundation that stabilizes with the roof that secures are two mighty pillars called *Stability* and *Strength*.

When King Solomon built the stunning temple in Jerusalem, he had Hiram of Tyre, a skilled bronze-worker, construct two massive columns to hold up the porch of the huge structure. One of the thick pillars was labeled *Jachin*, and the other, *Boaz* (1 Kings 7:21). They symbolized "stability and strength."[1] Together, they established security.

Jachin comes from a Hebrew word meaning "he will establish." The term *Boaz* is thought to be based on a word implying "strength."[2] God's temple, held up by "Stability" and "Strength," was a foreshadowing both of the church and the individuals who make it up (see Ephesians 2:21; 1 Corinthians 6:19).

YOUR CHILD'S A TEMPLE

Every human being is intended to be the temple of God, with his or her life secured on "Stability" and "Strength." Hiram of Tyre built the two pillars for Solomon's temple, but it's parents who must build these qualities early in their children's lives. The mothers and fathers who do that produce kids who are stable and secure when they become adults.

Built on Stability and Security?

If your son or daughter were eighteen and leaving home today to face the world, would you be able to say your child is stable and secure? If we live long enough, most of us will have the experience of a mother we'll call Karen. She arose one morning with tears pooling in her eyes after a fitful night of worrying about her daughter, Meagan. The summer following Meagan's high school graduation had zoomed by at warp speed. Now had come the day when Karen and her husband, Chuck, would put Meagan in the family car, drive her the 175 miles to the state university and return home without her.

Karen choked back the tears, not wanting to spoil this exciting day for Meagan. Her mind trekked back to the day two decades earlier when her own father had taken her to enroll in the same university. She had not been prepared for the onslaught that would batter her with gale-force winds in spirit, soul, and body. Karen remembered her dad driving that day in the silence that had characterized his entire relationship with his daughter. Her mother was at work, so she didn't accompany Karen and her dad to the university. With a wince, she thought of the lack of relationship, teaching, and spiritual values that had made her home at times seem like a flat, empty desert. And on this day when she was to deliver her own daughter into the hurricane of college life, Karen recalled the many mistakes she had made: the embarrassing arrest for drug possession, the abortion that had ended the life of her first child, the poor grades, and the wild sorority parties.

Ready for the Onslaught?

Things will be different for Meagan, Karen assured herself this day. At the precipice of a crashing marriage, Karen and Chuck had pulled back and committed their lives to Christ and biblical living. Through God's power, she and Chuck had escaped destruction. Karen whispered a prayer now, thanking God that the turnaround had come early in Meagan's life.

Meagan would sail out on the turbulent seven seas of spirituality, morality, human relationships, culture, academics, self-identity, and the choice of destinies. Would she be like a small boat bobbing in the heaving tides, or would Meagan be like a sturdy ship, well balanced on the bounding waves? Karen relaxed, knowing her daughter would go off to college with a different set of values and a stability and security that she herself had not known.

When a boat runs light on the water, it doesn't have enough weight to keep it balanced. Sailors put ballast in the hull to shove the craft down far enough that it rides the waves with stability. In the old days, cannon shot would be used or raw lead. Once, when the apostle Paul was en route to his trial in Rome, a storm slammed the ship he rode. In desperation, the crew dropped the sea anchors, hoping they would stabilize the vessel (Acts 27:17).

All the Meagans of the world— and their brothers—need the balancing ballast of God's Word and principles to stabilize them in the snarling currents that threaten to run them aground.

WAYS WE TRY TO MAKE OUR CHILDREN SECURE

Using a Spiritual "Full-Court Press"

Our children also need the strength that comes from security. There are varying approaches parents use when it comes to building stability and security into the lives of their children. First, there's what might be termed the *full-court press*. In basketball, defensive players will sometimes cover their individual opponents from the time the ball is tossed in bounds until it changes sides. Players employing the full-court press will be nose to nose, eye to eye with their counterpart all over the court, anticipating the opponent's actions rather than falling back slightly and waiting for the offensive player's moves.

Deuteronomy 6:6–9 describes a spiritual full-court press. Parents should etch God's Word into their own hearts, then teach their children "diligently." This relentless pursuit with truth should occur when parents and children are sitting together in their house, walking on the road—in twenty-first century parlance, driving to school or to soccer practice—when they're stretched out on their beds or lounge chairs, as well as when they get up. The Deuteronomy recommendation is that God's laws should be bound to the hand as a sign, attached to the forehead, and written on the doorposts of the house and the gates of the fence. No time-outs. Full-court press on every play.

The Deuteronomy passage lays out the principle of establishing an environment full of God's Word and truth. A family is to be saturated with the understanding of His principles for living. But Deuteronomy 6 is not a mandate for religious zealotry. The context of the whole Bible presents a lifestyle that flows naturally and logically from a loving relationship with God. Some parents, however, turn the passage into a prescription for religious fanaticism. Rather than nurturing their children with a healthy appreciation for God's truths, they foster a sinister dread of breaking religious rules.

They want to block every possibility of their child's moving into harm's way. Parents stuff their shelves with religious books; they take every Bible study available on Christian parenting; they play cassette tapes by biblical family counselors and teachers whether on short trips to the grocery store or long hauls during summer vacations.

To keep their son or daughter from being exposed to the world, these "hyperspiritual" parents build high, thick walls around the child. They shelter their kids from every influence deemed questionable. There's a tight list of acceptable friends, based on narrow criteria. Each child is force-fed on God, Jesus, the church, and the Bible. Children live a rule-bound, dour, confined existence.

Don't misunderstand; parents using the full-court press usually are well intentioned. But the religious flow they pump into their children during every waking moment is more than a child's capacity to receive.

Using the "Buffet" Approach

Other moms and dads embrace what might be termed the *buffet approach* to parenting. When it comes to what they will put on their child's mental and emotional platter, they are like people in a buffet line who dab a little blue cheese dressing on their salad, along with a smidgeon of ranch and thousand island dressings for added flavor. Standing before an array of meats, they pile on roast beef, some fried catfish, and a few turkey slices. Then the happy eaters load their plates with a dollop of mashed potatoes, a portion of creamed spinach, and a blossom of cauliflower drenched in cheese sauce. For dessert, there's fruit and chocolate cake and strawberry ice cream, with a forkful of coconut pie to "cleanse the palate."

In a buffet approach to parenting, parents back off religion in order to get their children out into the world to know its fare. Bible stories are replaced by *Harry Potter* and other tomes of the times. Every waking moment, the kids are involved in dance classes, ceramics, and athletic leagues. Buffet parents cram as much onto their child's plate as possible and then season it all with a dash of God—just enough for a balanced meal.

Using the Wisdom Approach and Its Two Principles

But there's a third parenting style—the *wisdom approach.* James 1:5 says if we lack wisdom, we can ask God, "who gives to all generously and without reproach, and it will be given to him." This is good news for parents, who need boxcars of wisdom.

PRINCIPLE ONE OF THE WISDOM APPROACH: FIND TEACHABLE MOMENTS

There are two principles in the application of divine wisdom in parenting. First is the principle of *teachable moments.* This relates to God's intended use for Deuteronomy 6. Rather than the full-court press, dads and moms following the teachable-moments strategy watch for those special times when their children are open and ready to hear and learn. Parents must be alert because these moments occur randomly—in the morning, evening, at mealtimes, or at play.

A teachable moment popped up one day at a baseball game for Richard and his son, Ricky. At nine, Ricky was learning to watch for good pitches. At the beginning of the season, Richard was pleased as his son kept his eye on the ball, leaned into the pitch, and swung the bat with all his power. As the season progressed, however, Ricky began pulling back from pitches, no matter how hittable they were.

"Son, you look like you're dodging the ball."

"Dad, I learned that if you lean into the pitch, you'll get hit," the boy replied.

Driving home, Richard used the event to teach his young son how life will throw some pitches that hurt, but that a person can't withdraw and become passive. He shared with Ricky important principles about "leaning into life," being alert for the things that hurt but not giving up.

Teachable moments come when a child has been hurt, but also when his behavior has come back to sting him—as when he has lied. They come when she has not been picked as a cheerleader, or he has been cut from the team. Teachable moments come with superior report cards and failing grades. They come when she doesn't have a date for the prom or isn't invited to the party of the season. I've discovered that the stages of development, when our children confront the physical and emotional changes in their lives, are wonderful instructive seasons. These are opportunities to teach our son or daughter deep principles and truths, such as grace, mercy, God's love, and the dynamics of sowing and reaping.

Through such teachable moments we show our children that God's truths are not true simply because they're in the Bible, but they are in the Bible because they *are* true.

Learning a Fundamental Worldview

A child who is learning principles in the crucible of life-experience grasps the fact that these standards are woven into the fabric of the universe, as surely and objectively as the law of gravity. If you utilize the teachable moments, you will lead your children in understanding that God's truths are essential and relevant to every dimension of their lives.

In this process, you are building into your children a worldview essential for the sense of stability and security in the chaotic, fallen world and its warped cultures. A worldview is the general outlook one has on life and all its experiences. It is a structure through which a person views reality. One individual will look at his environment and feel threatened and anxious. Another will look at the same vista and be happy and assured. The difference is in how the two individuals have been taught and conditioned to view reality.

Presuppositions are the building blocks of a worldview. These are the basic assumptions one makes, based on training and experience, of how life operates. For example, a child growing up in a poverty-stricken nation will assume life is a struggle and the world a cruel and bitter place. Another child, growing up in an upper-middle-class American suburb, might view life as a lark and the world as his toy.

An Important Exception

There is, however, an important exception: God can transform a person's faulty perspective. Tony was raised in a world of terror and violence, where both his parents used drugs. When they got "high," rather than becoming mellow, they fought viciously. Often one or both would wind up beating him. With his world always trembling on the brink of disaster, Tony struggled with paranoia and continual anxiety.

But as a man, Tony was noted by those who knew him best as a happy, solid citizen. He built a strong family and produced children who were confident and assured. What had made the difference? In his early teens, Tony had decided to rebel from his parents' lifestyle. If they were evil, he would be good. Tony sought a church and began attending with his friends. He became an avid Bible student.

Gradually, God's presuppositions began to push aside the old assumptions given through his parents, and Tony's worldview was slowly transformed. Rather than seeing reality through the shaky, frightened eyes of the circumstances in which he had been raised, Tony began to look at the world through the lens of God's Word. Up to that point, the only authority figures he had known were his parents. But as Tony received the truth that God is on the throne of the universe, it settled and reassured him.

Christ not only transforms corrupted behaviors, but also twisted worldviews! Though his parents didn't know—or care—about the wisdom approach, Tony found God's wisdom, and with it, stability and security. It's much better, much less painful, when a child doesn't have to stumble into the truths that will link the foundation and roof of his life, but instead has these principles built into his personality by strong parents who are using the teachable moments all along the way.

Understanding We Are Created for a Purpose

Such children grow up knowing they are the fruit of the creative hand of God. They have a sense that they have a message, made up of presuppositions and a worldview, that is unique and vital for the world, and that somehow they must share it. Children stabilized and secured on God's truth will know God created them for a purpose and be determined that the powers of darkness will not rob them of their life-mission. They will withstand temptation with greater resolve. These kids will be intelligent enough to know they are in the land of the dying but headed for the realm of the living.

The bottom line is they are developing a worldview of God, Jesus Christ, the Bible, the world, and everyday living that is coherent, with all the parts fitting together. They won't live those compartmentalized lives that set God's Word in one little corner and the world's presuppositions equally or greater in another. Rather, they will see their total life-experience in the context of reverencing God.

Such children, raised by the wisdom approach, will grow to function with wisdom. After all, "the fear of the Lord is the beginning of wisdom," says Proverbs 9:10. And, says Proverbs 2:1–8, there is a direct link between wisdom and stability and security:

My son, if you will receive my words and treasure my commandments within you, make your ear attentive to wisdom, incline your heart to understanding; for if you cry for discernment, lift your voice for understanding; if you seek her as silver, and search for her as for hidden treasures; then you will discern the fear of the Lord, and discover the knowledge of God. For the Lord gives wisdom; from His mouth come knowledge and understanding. He stores up sound wisdom for the upright; He is a shield to those who walk in integrity, guarding the paths of justice, and He preserves the way of His godly ones.

Parents who use the wisdom approach build the "temple" of their children's lives on foundations of granite. A category-five hurricane of trial and testing can't knock them down.

Amanda is a fifteen-year-old going on her first date. After a basketball game, about twenty kids are gathering at one of their homes. No chaperones will be present. Amanda's date, Ronny, is seventeen. The two are double-dating with Sherry, Amanda's best friend, also fifteen, and her boyfriend, Rick, who is sixteen. The foursome arrives at the party, where they dance, listen to music, and generally have a great time. All the boys are drinking a lot of beer, and a few of the girls are sipping with them.

Ronny signals Amanda, Sherry, and Rick to follow him into a back bedroom. There, he pulls out a marijuana cigarette and lights up.

"Ever tried this?" Ronny asks Amanda.

"No," she answers.

"Try it," Ronny says. "Just take one hit."

If Amanda has been brought up in a full-court press scenario with its legalism, hyper-pietism, and wall-like rigidity, chances are only fifty-fifty she will be stable enough to withstand the temptation. If she does resist, it likely will be because she is afraid of being caught and punished severely.

On the other hand, if Amanda has been raised on the buffet plan—a little dash of God and church, a little dash of sports, a little dash of everything—it's almost inevitable she will smoke the marijuana.

Avoiding Implosion

In fact, it's safe to say that a young person reared by either of those methods will implode when he or she gets to college. Kids brought up in the full-court press style will be away from the parental "Gestapo" for the first time. Frequently, they go wild. Young people nurtured at the buffet have been conditioned to believe they ought to give everything a try—and will.

What keeps Amanda from smoking the marijuana is that her parents used the wisdom approach in bringing up their daughter. She had a solid spiritual and moral foundation. Her parents had been highly sensitive in watching for and taking advantage of those God-appointed teachable moments through which they could shape a biblical worldview in Amanda's mind. They helped her think things through and arrive at her own conclusions about the priority of God in her life as she watched her parents' lifestyle. Her mom and dad's exemplary living was a critical factor in stabilizing and securing Amanda. Rather than blabbering with incessant preachiness, they lived in an unmistakable, shameless manner before their daughter.

Amanda withstood temptation not because she was worried about breaking rules but because the wrong behaviors were incompatible with the lifestyle nurtured in her upbringing. She would no more smoke a marijuana joint than she would write pornographic graffiti on a church wall. Amanda was secure in her own personality and the way she related to the world and had no inner need to defy her parents on the one hand nor, on the other, to sample everything on the buffet table. That security in her own identity provided the stability that kept Amanda from being crushed by temptation.

PRINCIPLE TWO OF THE WISDOM APPROACH: VIEW YOURSELF AS AN EQUIPPER

The second principle is that parents must see themselves as *equippers rather than transformers.* Such moms and dads build the double pillars of stability and strength at the threshold of their children's lives. A transformer parent looks at his child and says, "I'm going to straighten out that little brat." The equipper mother or father sees the child and says, "I'm going to build a temple."

Do You Have a Master Vision?

A man walking by a construction site asked a worker what he was doing. "Laying bricks," the man grunted back. The visitor asked another laborer what he was doing. "Earning a living," was the somber reply. Finally, the spectator put the question to a third workman. With excitement, the craftsman responded, "I'm building a cathedral."

Sadly, there are parents who are just laying the bricks when it comes to raising their children. They have no sweeping master vision of the life God has placed in their hands. Parenting to them is nothing more than putting food in the stomach and clothes on the body, while someone else puts education in the brain. Life is just a dull routine of laying one brick upon another until someone or something stops the process.

Other fathers and mothers see parenting as a duty, like the worker who was merely earning a living. The children are a burdensome responsibility, but someone has to perform the chore of raising them. Grimly, such parents take on the task because this is their lot in life.

Are You an Equipper or Transformer Parent?

The third worker symbolizes the equipper parent. Such mothers and fathers have a vision for the whole. They understand the world in which they are seeking to raise their children, and for which they must prepare their sons and daughters. Equipper parents see deep into the child, recognizing the bent of his personality, the rudimentary shapes of his gifts. Gently, moms and dads who equip their children encourage the direction of the personality's development and nurture the growth of the spiritual gifts. Most important, equipper parents have a huge perspective on God and His central role in their children's lives. They watch carefully for that age at which each child under their care—and it will be different for each— becomes aware of the difference between good and evil. Equipper parents point their children to the only Savior, Jesus Christ.

In contrast, transformer parents forget that it is God who does the transforming. Paul helped us get this clear when he wrote in 1 Corinthians 3:6, "I planted, Apollos watered, but God was causing the growth." Transformer parents take on the wrong job assignment. Rather than building temples with pillars of stability and strength into their children's lives, they build prisons.

Transformer parents tend to work from the outside to the inward. They try to produce change by punishing the body, or by giving external threats or manipulative tricks, assaulting the child's ears with condemning words or dominating decibels. B. F. Skinner and his armies of behavior modification experts are no different in objectives than the cruel father who beats his children. The only difference is in style. Both aim at conforming the child to the demands of the person in charge. Transforming parents produce a measure of short-lived compliance but never the deep, consistent commitment that makes a child stable and secure under the boisterous tornadoes of contemporary culture.

A LOOK AT POLYCARP'S PARENTS

In A.D. 155, Polycarp, the aged pastor of the church at Smyrna, was dragged to a post where he would be burned

for his service to Christ. Polycarp was given the chance to re-
nounce the Lord and save his life. Polycarp uttered one of
history's greatest replies: "Eighty-six years I have served Him
[Christ], and He has never done me wrong. How, then, should
I be able to blaspheme my King who has saved me?" Less
known is the fact that Polycarp grew up in a home under
equipper parents. They were led to Christ through Paul's ministry, and determined to raise their son as a man of God in
the midst of corrupting society. Rather than producing a child
who could give only resentful compliance, Polycarp's equipper parents produced a man of such commitment he could
be steady under the most severe threats and temptations.

Polycarp's parents positioned their son so that God could
transform and develop him.

God works from inward to outward. Under this arrange-
ment, the parents are "co-laborers" with God. They are the
equippers; He is the transformer. The dads and moms build
carefully, lovingly, and sensitively into their children's lives the
truths, principles, practical applications, and standards revealed in Scripture. The Holy Spirit joins this construction
team, taking the materials the parents place inside the temple they are building and cementing them solidly into the
child's life. God the Father has the master blueprint for each
individual and directs the laying of stone and brick upon the
foundation the parents have set, so that the appropriate transformation takes place.

DEEP INSIDE

Those who watch, like the man observing the three workers at the construction site, will not see everything that is un-
derway. The building progress is happening deep inside the
human being. Such children grow up in the profile of Ephesians 3:16–19, empowered from within.

Strengthened with power through His Spirit in the inner man, so that Christ may dwell in [their] hearts through faith; and that [they], being rooted and grounded in love, may be able to comprehend with all the saints what is the breadth and length and height and depth, and to know the love of Christ which surpasses knowledge, that [they] may be filled up to all the fullness of God.

If you're an equipper parent using the wisdom approach, your children will draw strength from within. In those scary moments when they are far away from the nest the first time, they will draw from their inner strength. They will do what comes "naturally," but that will be good, because what comes naturally for such a child will be the supernaturally cultivated character.

Many people cave in under temptation, testing, and trial because of feeling insecure and insignificant. They dash into multiple relationships looking for the love that signals acceptance and affirms their identity and personality. Such people get into financial trouble or tangle with the law in the attempts to make themselves significant in the eyes of another. Instability and insecurity plague their lives. The "porch" of their "temple" sags because they lack the forty-foot pillars with sufficient stability and strength to hold up the structure of their lives. It sounds simplistic, but the truth is confirmed day after day in the offices of psychotherapists and pastors, or on the stools of barrooms and the beds of illicit lovers. The bottom line for stability and security is love and acceptance.

FULFILLED NEED

Children embedded by equipper parents with the seed of God's love and who grow up nurtured in the awareness of His smile upon them don't have to spend their lives looking for love and acceptance. The need is fulfilled in their hearts by the only One who can fill that huge vacuum—the living God. No human being can meet that craving, so stable and secure people don't look for ultimate affirmation from other people. People raised under the wisdom approach by equipper parents don't have the need to hop from bed to bed or job to job. Their deepest love and affirmation needs are satisfied by the favor of God in their lives, with which the Holy Spirit fills them.

A child who learns his life is in the hands of God is steady and stable. Young Daniel wasn't hoodwinked by the fast-talking members of King Nebuchadnezzar's court in Babylon. Daniel knew who held his destiny, and it wasn't another human being. He couldn't be swayed by feasty foods from the palace kitchen or by threats of being hurled into fiery furnaces.

Children bathed in the knowledge that there is a purpose for their lives and that God is leading them according to plan become settled adults. They draw peace from knowing all things work together for good to them who love God and are called according to His purpose. They know that purpose is to bring them into Christlikeness within the fallen world (Romans 8:28–29). Such stable, secure people go through hard times like everyone else, but they don't give up, because they know all is proceeding according to plan—even if they don't understand it.

LEARNING FROM AUGUSTINE'S MOTHER

Monica, the mother of Augustine of Hippo—known to history as St. Augustine—was a great equipper parent. From the time Augustine was born in A.D. 354, Monica recognized that her son was an exceptional person. Initially, she tried to advance him socially and in a secular career. Monica, however, deepened in her own faith and became an equipper parent rather than a transformer mother. Meanwhile, her earlier efforts to motivate Augustine to grasp success in the world had taken hold. He scorned her new commitment to Christ. But

Monica wouldn't give up. She prayed consistently for her son, ministered Christ's love to him, and allowed God to be the transformer.

The strategy produced great fruit. In his *Confessions*, Augustine wrote of his mother, "In the flesh she brought me to birth in this world: in her heart she brought me to birth in Your eternal light."[3]

The most effective parents are those who build the pillars of stability and strength where they belong—at the "porch," the very threshold of life, as did the parents of Polycarp. But as Monica shows, even as the child matures, a parent can be a coworker with God in raising His glorious, sturdy temple of a human life.

QUESTIONS FOR PARENTS

1. As you consider your child's behavior, does he or she evidence the confidence that comes from security and strength?

2. What is the style in your home of reacting to emergencies and crises, and does that style nurture a sense of stability and strength or panic?

3. What is a recent or current "teachable moment" whereby you could establish your child in stability and strength?

4. What has been the prevailing approach to parenting in your home: "full-court press," "buffet-style," or "wisdom approach"? What do you need to change?

A PERSONAL WORD
Thou Shalt Have the Sex Talk with Thy Children

Even though this is the ninth commandment, I would guess this is the first chapter in this book many will read. It's time to deal with some of the most dreaded words of parenthood: "Mom, Dad, where did I come from?"

—E. Y.

THOU SHALT HAVE THE SEX TALK WITH THY CHILDREN

We've just learned that, as parents, we're in the temple-building business. Now it's time to direct our focus to the direct responsibility we have for helping our children maintain the purity of their "temples"—their bodies. That means parents must do what many find difficult: *They must have the "sex talk" with their children.*

Let's continue the temple analogy. Faithful Jews believed defilement of God's temple was among the most repugnant actions anyone could take. Their enemies knew trashing the temple was the ultimate insult and defeat for Israel.

Daniel the prophet foresaw a time when evil adversaries would swoop down on Jerusalem and set up in the temple the "abomination of desolation" (Daniel 11:31). The Hebrew word for "abomination" referred to something filthy and disgusting. Just about the most repulsive thing a faithful Jew could imagine would be the setting up of an idol in the Holy of Holies.

DEFILING GOD'S TEMPLE . . .
AND THE HUMAN TEMPLE

When Nebuchadnezzar and the Babylonians pummeled Jerusalem in 587–586 B.C., their greatest fury was reserved for the temple. They plundered its treasures, lit superheated fires, and reduced Solomon's work of art to ashes.

Under Zerubbabel, the temple was rebuilt and completed in 515 B.C., and it was remodeled and expanded by Herod almost five hundred years later. Yet this temple suffered the worst of abominations. The mad invader Antiochus Epiphanes not only took the temple's treasures in 169 B.C., but he sacrificed pigs on the high altar and set up a statue of Jupiter in the Holy of Holies. In A.D. 70, as Jesus had warned His disciples earlier, the Romans pulled down the temple of God and erected on its site a temple to Jupiter. Today, the ancient temple site is occupied by the Muslim Dome of the Rock.

The devil is passionate about defiling and destroying the temple of God—and that goes for the human temple too. In fact, the context of Paul's concern about defiling God's human temple in 1 Corinthians 6 is sexual immorality.

FORGETTING THE SACREDNESS OF SEX

As our Western society separates itself from its biblical roots, it loses the concept of the sacredness of sex. Culture redefines sexual morality and spins down into a whirlpool of sexual obsession. Down in this spinning maelstrom, the light of God's truth about sex is blocked out. The vortex of a godless culture accelerates spiritual and moral chaos. In no other facet of human existence is moral decay and depravity more evident than in that of sexuality.

Romans 1 describes the whirlpool of sexual immorality in stark terms:

For they exchanged the truth of God for a lie, and worshiped and served the creature rather than the Creator, who is blessed forever. Amen. For this reason God gave them over to degrading passions; for their women exchanged the natural function for that which is unnatural, and in the same way also the men abandoned the natural function of the woman and burned in their desire toward one another, men with men committing indecent acts and receiving in their own persons the due penalty of their error. (Romans 1:25–27)

NOTHING "SAFE" ABOUT IT

Down at the bottom of the tempest of perverted sexuality there is vast deception, more perhaps than in any other dimension of human existence. The code words of a sexually dysfunctional society—such as "safe sex"—become the propaganda elements by which the deception is advanced. The practitioners of deceit don't want people—especially the young—to know, for example, that no condom is 100 percent effective in preventing pregnancy or disease. They prefer to talk about the impracticality of abstinence programs and the need to teach young people how to implement "safe sex."

Yet the truth shows there is nothing "safe" for teenagers caught in the whirlpool.

In June 2003, the Heritage Foundation, a Washington think tank, released a study on adolescent sexuality.[1] About 48 percent of American high school youth have been or are sexually active, said the report, with often devastating consequences, like these:

- Daily, some 8,000 young people are infected with a sexually transmitted disease (STD), with a quarter of the nation's sexually active teens suffering from a STD.
- In the year 2000, some 240,000 babies were born to unwed mothers eighteen years of age and younger, most of whom faced a life of poverty and welfare dependency.

- Sexually active adolescents suffer more from depression than those not sexually active, said the Heritage report.

- Most frightening, the research found that sexually active teens are more likely to attempt suicide than those who aren't.

- Two-thirds of sexually active youth reported they wished they had waited until they were older before plunging into sexual encounters, with three-quarters of sexually active girls saying they regret not waiting.

The Heritage Foundation report stated that "early sexual activity is a substantial factor in undermining the emotional well-being of American teenagers."

Parents—we *must* have the sex talk with our children!

A "WHIRLPOOL" OF IMMORALITY

Frankly, those in the church, who ought to undergird parents in the moral development of their children, aren't much help. On the one hand, there is a pietistic wing that doesn't want to talk about sex. The other extreme found in the church is the trendy liberal wing that embraces the culture's perspective on sex rather than upholding the biblical worldview. But as entire societies plummet into the whirlpool of confused, chaotic, twisted sexuality, it's time for the church to speak out!

The church has the mission of ministering God's Word to the world. Only through biblical revelation can people understand and rightly utilize this sacred and powerful gift from God.

Proverbs tells us how we got into this whirlpool: "His own iniquities will capture the wicked, and he will be held with the cords of his sin. He will die for lack of instruction, and in the greatness of his folly he will go astray" (Proverbs 5:22–23). Many have dipped their toe into the water of casual or recreational sex only to be tugged into the riptide that is so deadly to physical, mental, emotional, and spiritual health, and so destructive to families and societies. Why?

The key to the answer, according to the proverb, is that people "die for the lack of instruction." One generation fails to teach their children about the wonderful and sacred gift of biblical sexuality. So the next generation fails to provide instruction, and then the next . . . until those who follow sink into ever-deepening murkiness. Therefore, in the realm of human sexuality, rather than truth and light, darkness, decay, and deception reign.

THE SEX "EDUCATORS"

In an earlier chapter, we stressed that if we don't teach our children, someone else will. In no other area of our kids' lives is this truer than with regard to sex. The truth is, *others are teaching our* children!

- *The media teach our children.* Television bombards youth with 15,000 sexual images annually.[2] No wonder a British organization found that 64 percent of adults think children learn about sex "from popular culture, television and magazines."[3] The numbers probably wouldn't vary much for the United States. About 75 percent of the music videos shown on MTV are loaded with sexual content, 50 percent with violence, and 80 percent with a mix of the two.[4] In fact, 70 percent of American teens get their sex information primarily from media.[5]

- *Teachers instruct our children about sexuality.* Schools try to take on the role of sex educator, but since the biblical moral view is banished from public education, the schools teach a largely valueless approach emphasizing pregnancy and STD prevention, and sexual technique. Eddie Ferguson, leader of the British organization cited

177

above, could have been speaking about American public schools as well when he said, "It's no longer sufficient for a teacher to be an expert in his/her subject. Increasingly we are expected to impart the social and civic skills which are fundamental to the smooth running of a democratic society; skills which, not so long ago, were transmitted by the family, the churches, and the community."[6]

- *Peers teach children about sex.* In fact, teens themselves report they get most of their information about sex from their peers.[7] It may be because some youth find their parents silent on the topic, unwilling to discuss it. Often, the sex "education" from their peers consists of a mix of outright lies, half-truths, and a few tidbits of truth. Some parents aren't able to help because they learned about sex from their own peers.

Parents on both sides of the Atlantic seem to look to professionals to inform their children about human sexuality. Ironically, of the adults interviewed for the British report, only 36 percent thought it to be the parents' task to instruct their children about sex. It's no better in America. The U.S.-based National Campaign to Prevent Teen Pregnancy found that one in five kids *under fourteen* have had sex. "What is really clear from this report," said Michael Resnick of the University of Minnesota, "is that it's still the voices of parents and other adults that are stunningly absent in the lives of many of our kids."[8]

Again, *if you don't teach your children about sex, someone else will.* Further, the information being pumped into children by all the other sources is contributing to the darkness, decay, and deception about sex. Parents with a Bible-shaped vision can give their kids truth and light that will displace the darkness and deception.

PARENTS AND "THE TALK"

Many parents would rather kiss a cobra on the head than have the sex talk with their children. For such dads and moms, the five most frightening words they will ever hear from their child are, "Where did I come from?" Those brave parents who try to answer the question often feel they failed. Still, they are to be congratulated for making the attempt.

It's crucial to know when to have the sex talk with our children. There is no set age, because children vary in their rates of maturity. We must be sensitive to the development of our kids—physically and psychologically. There are, however, some guidelines for various age categories.

Ages One to Five Years

Ages one through five represent the season for laying the groundwork. During these early years, children are information-eaters. Words, concepts, and visual relationships pour into their brains by the thousands. This is the point where parents should teach children names for body parts. It's funny how we use all the right words—an ear is an ear, a nose a nose—until we get to the genitals. Then we make up all sorts of labels for the private parts. But a penis is a penis, and a vagina, a vagina. The new name made up by the parent is no improvement on the actual terms. So parents should call the organs what they are.

The early stage of a child's life is also the time when a dad and mom should be teaching their children the truth that the body is a gift from God. Young children should be taught the worldview that their body is special because it's God's house on earth, and therefore, it's good.

When our oldest son, Ed, was in prekindergarten, his teacher became pregnant. Every afternoon he would report that Mrs. Rogers was "getting bigger and bigger." Jo Beth reassured him that sometimes mothers put on a pound or two, and that Mrs. Rogers would be fine.

As the weeks went by, Ed's concern grew. Jo Beth talked to me about it, and I performed that famous male maneuver known as "passing the buck." I told her that if Ed asked again, she would have to tell him something that would satisfy him.

Ed did ask again, so Jo Beth explained, "Mrs. Rogers is going to have a baby, and it's growing inside her. At just the right time, the baby will come out."

"Does the baby have a blanket in there?" he asked.

"No," replied Jo Beth, "it's kept warm by its mommy's body, and it has plenty of food to eat."

Ed's little face was cloaked suddenly in deep contemplation. "Did I grow up in you like that?" he asked Jo Beth.

"Yes, son, you surely did." Jo Beth felt relieved. She had finally given our little son the straight of it. Quickly, though, her satisfaction was punctured.

With utter conviction, Ed looked her squarely in the eye and announced, *"I don't believe it!"* End of discussion—for that moment anyway.

However, Jo Beth deserved a gold star for openness. Though Ed was unconvinced, she sought to be honest and to answer his questions plainly, gently, and gladly. Such an attitude takes the brown wrapper off the sex topic and allows the children to know it's not a taboo subject. Later in life, they're not afraid to come to their parents with larger questions about sex.

Ages Six to Nine

Youngsters are growing up fast during ages six through nine. This is the stage when they should begin to hear about reproduction and basic facts of life suitable to their age. Children today in this age range already are hearing about sex from their peers. They scan cable TV channels and see the images scattered over the airwaves by a sex-manic culture. Kids in this category must get the truth about sex before they start paying attention to the distortions.

Find out what your child already knows. Clear up any misinformation. Establish your word as reliable, true, and informed so he doesn't have to get his information elsewhere. Don't be afraid of questions. Keep the topic on a positive note: Sex is a gift from God, a positive part of life, and He has the plan and directions for its use.

Ages Ten to Thirteen

When children are ages ten to thirteen, the information flow narrows from a broad river to frothing whitewater. The sex talk should become specific and focused. Difficult topics and terms come into the conversation, like *menstrual flow, masturbation,* and *wet dreams.* Parents must prepare their boys and girls for puberty and the changes that will thunder over their bodies.

Kids at this stage don't need a professor but a pal, a fellow traveler who has walked this strange road and can point the way. So screen out the dry academics from your sex-talk repertoire and remember when you were once an adolescent. Think about the feelings you may have experienced—shame, confusion, curiosity, fear. Head off those emotions in your child.

Treat the sex talk like a feast. The appetizer is the good news that human beings are "fearfully and wonderfully made." The salad is the fact that God has a terrific plan for the child's life. The main course is the teaching about the details of sex, the relation of sexual behavior to purity, the corruptions of fornication and adultery, the role of the body as the temple of God, and the actualization of God's plan for the individual. The dessert is the positive word about the pleasure of sex in marriage, performed by God's pattern.

Ages Fourteen to Eighteen

Getting kids ready to date is the sex-talk objective at ages fourteen to eighteen. The primary adolescent years are the season when moms and dads should discuss dating, "petting" (i.e., sexual touches), and the pressures that come from being out with the opposite sex. Girls need to get prepped on how to snip the famous line many hear inevitably: "If you love me, you'll do it." A young man needs coaching on how to pour cold water on a sizzling date that comes on to him. Both need to learn to respect the opposite sex.

Teenagers expect honesty and frankness from their parents. A story about a parent's own experience is much better than a languid theological lecture or sociological essay. I have a friend who used the personal testimony approach with a surprising outcome.

"You can overcome temptation, because I did," my friend told his teenage son. Then the dad recounted the story of being on a business trip with his boss and a beautiful secretary handpicked for the journey. My friend was responsible for processing and finalizing reports and agreements resulting from each day's discussions. The secretary would come to his room at the close of business each day, where her typewriter (it was long ago) was set up.

One afternoon, she came into the room and slipped into my friend's bed. When he realized what was going on, he dashed from the motel room so quickly he left a small whirlwind behind, along with an insulted blond.

Twenty years later, my friend and his son—now thirty—were on an airplane together. At Albuquerque, a stunning woman boarded the flight. My buddy looked closer and realized it was the woman he had been telling his son about. The dad was sitting in an aisle seat, and the woman sat just across from him.

When my friend and his son landed and disembarked, the

father said, "Son, do you remember how I told you I overcame temptation those many years ago?"

The young man rolled his eyes, thinking his dad was about to launch off on the story one more time. "Yeah, Dad, I remember."

"Well, that woman sitting next to me on the plane was the very woman who got in my bed!"

The son's eyes looked like cue balls on a billiard table. "Wow, Dad, she was really beautiful. It must have taken tremendous strength to run away from her!"

FACE TO FACE

My friend later reflected on how he would have felt about the chance encounter in the presence of his son had he succumbed two decades earlier. The father was grateful he could set a positive example. My friend was even more grateful God had brought him and his boy face to face with the temptation he had overcome years ago. He knew his son would never forget it and would be better equipped to talk to his own son about sex.

Obviously, many parents did not overcome temptation when they were teenagers. They need to teach out of that experience too. In addition to stories of hurt, guilt, and haunting memories, they can teach about God's grace and His call to a higher, pure life.

Sex is not, after all, the required rite of passage into adulthood. It's thrilling to see more and more teens pledging to remain pure sexually until their wedding. Robert Rector, senior research fellow of the Heritage Foundation recently reviewed studies of ten sexual abstinence programs. He concluded, "True abstinence programs help young people develop an understanding of commitment, fidelity and intimacy that will serve them well as the foundations of healthy marital life in the future."[9]

Rector also found that parents are vital in helping teens follow through with their pledge. Reporting the findings of the National Longitudinal Study of Adolescent Health, Rector wrote, "When taking a virginity pledge is combined with strong parental disapproval of sexual activity, the probability of initiation of sexual activity is reduced by 75 percent or more."[10]

A "PROMISING CHUNK" OF GOOD NEWS

AIDS is killing so many people in Africa that President Bush has focused American resources on helping solve the problem. Yet buried in the mire of negative reports is a promising chunk of good news. In Uganda, the HIV infection rate fell from 30 percent of the population in the 1990s to only about 10 percent a decade later. The reason was that, with the blessing of the government and the wife of Uganda's president, a "True Love Waits" campaign was launched to encourage young people to abstain from sex until marriage. While such success through sexual abstinence goes largely unreported, in many nations young people are discovering that true love really does and can wait.[11]

In my book *Pure Sex,* I noted three things held in common by teenagers who choose to reserve sex for marriage.[12] First, these young people *see themselves as unique people* with a special contribution to make to the world. Someone—a parent, teacher, friend, or relative—has fired these kids with a vision of their own value. They are secure in the knowledge they are loved, because that love has been actualized and demonstrated by people significant to these youth. They have learned to see themselves as God does, as precious and infinitely valuable.

Second, teenagers committed to waiting until marriage *have a reverence for God and His principles.* They are not afraid to say no. Someone taught them right and wrong as absolutes at a young age. They refuse to buy into situational ethics and movable morality. They have solid standards. Like young Daniel in Babylon, they have set their mind not to veer from their principles (see Daniel 1:8).

Finally, teenagers choosing to wait until marriage to have sex *prize others' worth*. They don't regard other human beings as their personal toys or objects of gratification. Kids who abstain respect the needs and feelings of other people, and value them as being as important as their own.

OK—IT'S TIME FOR "THE TALK"

Now that we understand our need to talk to our children about sex throughout the various stages of their lives, let's consider how to have these crucial conversations. The content and methodology of the sex talk at each level is vital.

The Talk Before the Talk

The *first step* is "the talk before the talk." This lays the groundwork and consists of the worldview we live openly before our children daily. Paul wrote that we are to "work out" our salvation (see Philippians 2:12). What we believe in the holy of holies of our life-temple is to become evident in our behavior and actions. The biblical worldview parents ought to display to their children has these elements:

- God created the world.
- This God who created the world created you and me.
- This God who created the world and you and me created us for a divine purpose and has a plan for our lives.
- It is possible to know God, as well as His purpose and plan for our lives.
- He leads us to accept His free gift of salvation by receiving His Son Jesus Christ into our lives.

This worldview provides a comprehensive understanding and sets a context for practical living. Children growing up in a home permeated with this biblical outlook are established on a solid foundation. They flourish in a loving atmosphere. Watching mom and dad love God and each other builds security and confidence into children's lives. They become the direct recipients of this unshakable, unconditional love as parents pour it into them through words, touching, holding, rocking, and playing from birth through the teen years. Positive messages about human sexuality and sexual behavior bloom naturally on such a stem. The child is picking up feelings, emotions, insights, passions, and motives that will be the elements of his sexual concepts as he matures.

"Kissing the Cobra"

The *second step* in the sex talk is the "talk" itself. Here now is the face-to-face encounter many parents dread, the moment for kissing the cobra on the head. Remember, the age at which a parent has this talk depends on the age and readiness of the child. In the sex talk, parents must *tell it like it is*. The age at which a child can handle the straight information will vary, so again, parents need to be sensitive.

Here is a helpful outline for the sex talk—just fill in each point with your own words:

    I. God's first command to human beings was to reproduce and scatter all over the earth so they could enjoy what God created. (Show the child that sex is God's idea.)

    II. God gave this command to one man and one woman, who, together, constituted a marriage. (Discuss the difference between heterosexual and homosexual behavior, and why the Bible opposes homosexuality.)

    III. God gave them the gift of sex so they could reproduce.

(Describe sex as God's gift and explain the details of reproduction.)

IV. God also gave the gift of sex so a husband and wife could express their love and oneness and enjoy intimacy with one another. (Help the child understand the importance of marriage and how sex outside marriage is ultimately harmful and wrong.)

V. Above all, God gave the gift of sex as an illustration of the relationship between God and His bride—the church; therefore, sex between a husband and wife is sacred. (Talk about how God shares His intimate love with us.)

VI. When Adam and Eve chose sin, they corrupted God's beautiful gift of sex, so it's important for us to allow God's Word to be the standard for our sexual behavior. (Discuss the crisis of sex outside marriage, including fornication and adultery, the dangers of sexually transmitted diseases, the tragedy of illegitimacy, the failure of the "living together" relationship, the horror of abortion, and the destruction of the family. Note also that *not* "everybody is doing it." If 48 percent of American high-school teens report being sexually active, 52 percent—more than half—aren't!)

VII. God's grace extends forgiveness when we violate His standards for sexual behavior. (Through David's adultery, show the child how sex outside God's standards has tragic consequences but how God forgives and restores us to Himself.)

The Talk After the Talk

Step three of the sex talk is "the talk after the talk." Actually, these are *talks*. There will be ongoing conversations between parents and children, especially as social borders and relationships expand.

Dads and moms must do more than continue verbalizing, however—they must be involved in their children's lives. Parents can continue to have a strong influence over their kids as they mature, but it requires interacting with and participating in their children's experiences.

KEEP THE LINES OPEN

This means keeping the communication lines open. As children enter the teen years, the channels for interaction between them and their parents get clogged. Peer expectations, feelings that parents don't understand, the inability to articulate what they're feeling, and their own confusion comprise the gunk kids place in the communications pipeline.

Parents add their own stifling stuff: anger, mistrust, fear, inability to relate, and their own self-doubt as they age. Nevertheless, the burden is on the mother and father to unclog the communications link between themselves and their teenage offspring. Here are some tips for doing that:

- *Schedule special times.* A mother might schedule a periodic, regular shopping day with her teenage daughter, including lunch. A father could take his son hunting, fishing, or to a sports event. Dads ought to take out their daughters, and moms should schedule special times with their sons too. The point is not to force conversation but to provide a forum where talk and interaction will flow smoothly and naturally.

- *Ask advice from your teen.* This sounds like a shocker, but nothing will show your respect for your teenager like asking his or her opinion. This can include everything from their feelings about your dress (get ready to be insulted) to their views of politics and candidates. In fact, ask your teen for his or her opinion on substantive issues, then sit back and listen.

- *Involve the teen in family decisions.* This narrows down and raises the ante on the teenager's opinion, since it deals with issues impacting family life. The teenager now begins to assume some responsibility for the family lifestyle and activities by being given an opportunity for input.

- *Discover dreams and aspirations.* Ask your child what he wants out of life and how you can help him achieve it. Nurture and elevate his or her aspirations by encouraging the teen to reach for the highest. Talk about life purpose, mission, and goals, and help your son or daughter set them.

While all these topics may not deal directly with sex, they keep the channels open so that when the continuing sex talk needs to occur—either at their initiative or yours—the communication line is clear and ready.

In fact, moms and dads who work to maintain an open link for the "talk after the talk" find they can present the hard facts without their teens seeing the conversations as preachy sermons. For youngsters traveling at warp speed through the intense hormonal changes and sexual curiosity of adolescence, there's a great need to be brought down to earth by the hard truth of sowing and reaping, actions and consequences.

THE STRAIGHT FACTS

Parents who keep the lines open can tell their teenagers these hard, honest facts: that those who are sexually active before marriage have a higher rate of depression and suicide, that unwed mothers are often doomed to poverty, that live-together mates have a higher divorce rate than those who wait, along with all the other evidence showing the consequences of fornication and adultery. A dad who keeps the lines open with his teenage son can tell him that sex outside marriage is a losing lifestyle. A mother with a clear communication channel to her daughter can help her understand that a sexual relationship outside marriage is a guarantee for heartbreak.

Dads and moms who stay involved can lead their teenagers to see that practitioners of sex outside marriage lose their freedom, their joy, and often their lives—at least the high purpose for which God brought them into the world.

The greatest music to an aging parent's ears is composed and sung by an adult child who says ultimately, "Dad . . . mom, you were right. Thank you for telling me the truth when I was young."

Parents who hear that melody are listening to a replay of the tune they themselves sang into their kids' lives years before, when they cared enough to have the sex talk.

QUESTIONS FOR PARENTS

1. Where did you get your first information about sex?
2. What misconceptions do you think children growing up today have about sex, and how will you correct those misconceptions for your children?
3. If you made sexual mistakes when you were growing up, what will you say to your children now?
4. If you remained abstinent when you were growing up, what will you say to your children now?

A PERSONAL WORD
Thou Shalt Not Be a Passive Parent

If a permanent record were kept for parents like there is for students, how many absences would you have, mom and dad? Are you available and involved in your child's life? If not, you're raising a child doomed for difficulty . . . and you're missing out on life's treasures.

—E. Y.

Commandment 10

THOU SHALT NOT
BE A PASSIVE PARENT

A strange contradiction prevails among many fathers and mothers living in our high-speed, ambition-driven, activist-oriented Western world: Though spurred by high-energy initiative in their careers and lifestyles, they become practitioners of what might be termed "nirvana parenting."

What do I mean by that? "Nirvana parenting" is a passive, remote-controlled type of parenting, grounded in Buddhist teaching and Eastern mystical influence. In the 1960s, many young people who would become parents during the 1970s and 1980s became enamored with Eastern mysticism, with its emphasis on "detachment" from pain and suffering as the highest goal of salvation. The worldview of Zen Buddhism—with its strong emphasis on do-it-your-way, intensely individualized spirituality—grew into a giant tide sweeping along many of the elite opinion-makers whose influence on the spiritually-seeking would linger.

SATURATED WITH BUDDHISM

Indeed, many Americans separated from their biblical roots as they read books, articles, academic studies, and pop psychology. Meanwhile movies and TV shows saturated society with the three concepts of Buddhism: Everything is "impermanent," material things are "insubstantial," and "nirvana is quiescence."[1]

The great goal for many rootless spiritual nomads became *nirvana*. For the Zen Buddhists, this means a disinterest that enables a person to have wisdom and compassion, yet not be troubled by nagging emotions and feelings that come with worry and concern. Hindus see nirvana as emancipation from attachments.

The term literally means "a blowing out." Nirvana is the extinguishing of passions and cravings, and "liberation" from all limitations. It is soaring out over problems and needs through a belief they are not real. For its adherents, nirvana "is the supreme goal of human existence."[2]

As it percolated through Western culture, Zen, nirvana, and other Eastern concepts lost some of their defining traditions and meanings and dripped out as mere *passivity*. Its mantra, repeated daily by millions, is *"Whatever . . . "*

Nirvana-Zen concepts permeated and poisoned public education. Every child was his own little universe and should be allowed to learn at his own pace. Grade inflation, collapsing academics, and school systems with their own police forces were the result.

THE "HIGH PRIEST" OF NIRVANA PARENTING

The history of nirvana parenting can be traced to the teachings of Benjamin Spock more than a half century ago. He became the high priest of nirvana parenting. His *Common Sense Book of Baby and Child Care* first appeared in 1946; it would sell more than 50 million copies. Spock fed American parcnts a sour stew mixed with thought from Rousseau and Freud with some nirvana-type detachment thrown in. Rather than interfering with children's instinctive, often aggressive, behaviors, parents should focus on their instinctive needs, Spock preached.

The 1960s saw the first crop of Spock-raised babies, and, after observing them and just before his death, Spock apologized for his ideas. They were merely hypotheses, he said, not proven by experience.

Nevertheless, in the 1970s, Dr. Thomas Gordon took the Spockian notions to a new level. *The New York Times* once described his Parent Effectiveness Training (PET) as a "national movement." By 1976, thousands of parents were studying Gordon's concepts in some eight thousand classes scattered throughout the nation. Gordon admonished mothers and fathers to reject authority in dealing with their children, allow children to set their own limitations, and find "nonpower" methods for interacting with their kids.

The kids raised on *Common Sense*, PET, and the Zen-nirvana principles of these two men grew up and had children whom they raised as they had been. Ultimately, the concept was tagged as "permissive parenting."

"PASSIVE PARENTING"

A better way to describe permissive parenting is *"passive parenting."* Such moms and dads sit by, like happily oblivious Buddhas squatting under a banyan tree while their kids wreak havoc.

Isaac, father of Jacob and Esau, was a passive parent. Genesis 25:28 sums it up. "Now Isaac loved Esau, because he had a taste for game, but Rebekah loved Jacob." The sibling rivalry energized by this parental division of affections brought turmoil to Isaac's house. Fights, arguments, and deceptions were the normal family routine. Isaac wasn't dumb, and knew what was going on. But he was passive, detached, uninvolved—a nirvana devotee long before Buddha!

Passivity is a paradox. You would think it would just fade away. Instead, passivity droops into an ever-deepening void, with each generation sinking lower—as the outcome of Spock-parenting showed. Jacob continued the trend and did more damage because he had more children than Isaac. Incest, murder, rape, and deception characterized his household. Jacob's kids had so much sibling rivalry they sold one of their brothers, Joseph, into slavery. Jacob knew these things were going on but, aside from an occasional mild rebuke, did nothing about it.

There's hardly a greater indictment that can be brought against parents than to say they are passive. Specifically, I'm talking about dads and moms who don't seem to care about being spiritual leaders in their homes. So we have the schizoid home where the parents are Western activists when it comes to music lessons, soccer games, art classes, and dance recitals, but Eastern nirvana-practitioners when it comes to giving spiritual leadership.

SAYING "WHATEVER"

The same parent who will repolarize the planet to get a child to a ballgame will say, *"Whatever,"* when it comes to giving direction about church attendance or the child's choice of spiritual belief.

Parents who function like this are operating under the curse, like Isaac and Jacob. When Adam and Eve dined on the forbidden fruit, they climbed up on the throne of their lives and shoved God aside. They now had His knowledge, they figured, so they could run their own lives. *Wrong.* They found out in a hurry they weren't equipped for God's job description.

Life's really big question ever since has been, *Who's in charge?* The curse is all about you and me trying to be in control rather than God. The fundamental temptation is power. Original sin (and all its sprouts) is about control. And here's the irony of passivity: *The more we try to take control, the more we try to get out from under control.* Isaac and Jacob and all passive parents want the freedom to do their own thing. Children interfere with that "freedom" to be in control. Passive parents are unwilling to pay the price of building the right stuff into their kids. It robs them of freedom to pursue their self-interests, demands discipline, and places controls on their schedules and priorities. Passive parents actually are under the control of the doctrine that says that their personal fun, privileges, lifestyle, careers, and agenda are more important than raising healthy, whole children.

THE MYTHS THAT PASSIVE PARENTS BELIEVE

What possible rationale could parents give for not being spiritual leaders and genuine fathers and mothers to their children? How can a passive parent bear to look in the mirror? Such moms and dads are able to justify their attitudes because they've bought into certain modern myths.

Myth 1: The "Good" Bad Child

The notion of a "good" bad child has been woven into our culture by such spinners as Mark Twain and his lovable characters Tom Sawyer and Huck Finn, or by Hank Ketchum and his Dennis the Menace. In fact, we could call this myth the Dennis the Menace Syndrome. All these characters do bad things, but they are so cute carrying out their mischief that it makes them "good."

Our children, many of us think, may be Dennis the Menaces, inflicting the world's Mr. Wilsons with untold misery, but somehow they will turn out okay. Not to worry. Go sit under the banyan tree. Trip off into nirvana. *"Whatever . . ."*

Myth 2: The "Natural Good"

Jean-Jacques Rousseau, the eighteenth-century French philosopher, and a herd of his disciples promoted the illusion that people are basically good and are corrupted by the bad things in the environment in which they were raised. Babies emerge from their mothers' wombs as "blank tablets." There's no messy sin nature, just an empty slate. Raise them in a pristine paradise, and they will be good always.

The passive parent concludes the best strategy is to stay out of the kid's way and let him flow through life, unobstructed. If nature is allowed to take its course, the child will choose the right path. *"Whatever . . ."*

Myth 3: The Evil of (Parental) Imposition

"Who am I to impose my beliefs on my children?" asks the parent swallowing this bait. Such fathers and mothers advocate total democracy in the home. The child not only gets a vote, but in many cases has the *only* vote. If she wants to have sex as a teen, at least let her use her own bedroom. If he and his friends want to drink or get high, let them have the pot party at home, off the streets. If the child wants to poster his walls in demonic images, let him do so. If the daughter decides to worship a pink mushroom, it's her choice.

Such passive parents have been skewered on the scam. While they're not imposing their beliefs on their children, society is pumping these children nonstop with its belief systems and lifestyles. Passive parents don't impose their beliefs on their kids but turn them over to the toxic culture to indoctrinate them. *"Whatever . . ."*

TELLING CHILDREN
THEY'RE UNIMPORTANT

While passive parents swallow the myths, they also promote the idea that their children are unimportant. A child asks for a certain item, and the mom snaps, "We can't afford that!" No reason nor explanation. "Sit down and be quiet!" a dad yells at his son. "I'm too tired" is the lament many a child hears from a passive parent. All these excuses convey to children the message that they aren't important.

By the way, the three statements listed above, among the most frequent children hear, are often true. The family budget is limited, children do need to behave, and parents get tired. Most all of us—including me—have used these litanies. They are not bad in themselves. The problem comes when we offer no other explanation to the child or fail to provide information. A caring parent would say, "Honey, we can't afford that new toy right now because this is the week in our budget we have to pay our monthly house payment." A dad concerned for the impact of his words will correct his interrupting son by telling him there will be an opportunity for him to speak later. A weary but thoughtful mother will tell her child that she's too tired to go out now for a pizza, but as soon as she rests a bit, she'll discuss the possibility. The passive parent won't take the time to provide explanations and will convey the notion to the child that he or she isn't important enough to be considered.

"POSSESSIVE PARENTING"

The polar opposite of passivity is possessiveness. It's just as destructive. Possessiveness pops up in a variety of ways—even in parental leniency. For example, Jack fell into lust (not love!) with his secretary, parted ways with his wife, and now lives with the secretary. Jack and Jill get a divorce. Jill receives custody of the kids, and Jack gets visitation rights. Bobby and Sally, Jack and Jill's kids, get to stay with their father and the secretary every other weekend, according to the settlement. Jack, consumed with guilt for the impact of the divorce on his kids, becomes an "anything-you-want" dad. The kids think he's the greatest . . . and why wouldn't they? Every other weekend they enjoy a theme-park lifestyle and are surrounded by the latest and greatest toys and gadgets—all supplied by their dad, Jack.

Then it's back home to Jill. Chores and homework await Bobby and Sally there. Jill oversees the monotonous daily routine. She frets that she is now the heavy in her kids' lives and decides to lighten up so Bobby and Sally will love her as much as they do Jack. Now Bobby and Sally have two equally lenient, indulgent parents, and no discipline.

No wonder God hates divorce (Malachi 2:16) . . . and so should we! He loves the divorced person but hates divorce and the sin that led to it. Former mates must sit down and reason together biblically and intelligently regarding the rearing of their children. Pride and ego must go. Popularity struggles have to be set aside. "Exes" must jettison the negative attitudes and opinions with which they're propagandizing their kids about one another. There is only one issue: what is best for the children.

Possessive parents are so "activist," so involved, so intertwined with their child's life that the son or daughter hardly has breathing room. Much has been written about the "cheerleader mom" in the Houston area where I live, but little about the impact of the possessive mother's action on the daughter. You may recall the mother who wanted her child to make the cheerleading squad so intensely that she tried to get rid of the competition just about any way she could. This mother was by no means a passive parent!

Ephesians 6:4 has a warning and advice for both passive and possessive parents. "Fathers, do not provoke your children to anger; but bring them up in the discipline and instruction of the Lord," says the verse. "Fathers" is a generic term here, referring to both parents. Passive and possessive parents provoke their children to wrath. Passive parents do so through their neglect and devaluing of the child. Possessive moms and dads provoke children through their suffocating indulgence on the one hand and unyielding grip on the other.

"PARTICIPATIVE PARENTING"

Rather than being passive or possessive, biblical parenting is *participative*. Dads and moms following this style participate with their children and provide opportunities for their children to participate with them in activities and decisions. Participative parents are not dominating, but neither are they run over by their kids.

The advice in Ephesians 6:4 gives direction for the participative parenting style. It deals with God's discipline and instruction. These are vital elements in participative parenting. I call this the "Triple 'A' Secret."

Affirmation

The first "A" is *affirmation*. Fathers, especially, must affirm their children. A supernatural relationship exists normally between mothers and their offspring. Mom carried the baby nine months in her womb, so the bond between mother and child was established from conception. Dads must work at building this quality of supernatural relationship. Affirmation is a vital tool to help a father be a true participative parent. A child needs to hear his dad say, "I'm proud of you." A young man needs to feel his father's respect over a particular achievement, and a young lady needs to know that in her dad's eyes she is beautiful.

Fathers need to join mothers in tucking in their kids at night. They need to speak words of strong affirmation as the last thing a child hears before drifting off to sleep, words like, "You're exactly what I would have ordered if I could have special ordered you from God!"

The classic comedian Eddie Cantor once said that every

time he looked at the FBI's Ten Most Wanted List, he always thought, "If we'd made them feel wanted earlier, they wouldn't be wanted now." Let your kids know they are on your "wanted list" by affirming them, and perhaps they won't be on a "wanted list" later in life!

Appreciation

The second "A" is *appreciation*. Even the youngest children need to know they are appreciated. I always enjoy hearing and watching when young children sing in our worship services—particularly our preschoolers. I usually scan the parents more than the kids. I especially get a delight out of watching parents send signals to their children on stage.

A little girl, about five, ran up to her daddy after a service in which she had sung. I watched as she grabbed her father's leg as he spoke with another parent. She looked up at him, and started to say something. "Susan," he snapped back, "be quiet! Can't you see I'm trying to talk here?" Honestly, I had to fight the compulsion to walk over to that dad and say, "You're too stupid to be a parent!" True, children need to learn manners. But that father sent his daughter a message that said the conversation with the other adult was more important than she. At her age, this was likely the first time the little girl had performed in public. All she wanted was her dad to tell her how wonderful she had been.

Up there in the clouds where the father and the other person conversed, there was little awareness of how the little girl "down below" saw the world. Maybe the dad would have understood if he had come down to his daughter's level. If the father had been on trial for ignoring his daughter, a fitting punishment would have been to require the dad to walk around on his knees for a week. Parents who get on their children's level learn to appreciate the child's perspective. They learn the importance of expressing that appreciation. Had that dad spent a week looking at the world at his daughter's level, instead of cutting her off, he might have said something like, "You were wonderful! I'm so proud of you! You knew just about every word in the song!"

Affection

The third "A" is *affection*. I have always shown my affection to our three sons by kissing them—even now, though they are grown men. In our culture, many men have a problem showing such affection to their children, especially their boys.

"My friends think it's weird when you kiss me in front of them," a teen told his father.

"Okay, we'll substitute a 'high five' for the kiss," answered the dad.

That's what they did, because the father didn't want to embarrass his son, but he did want to show his growing teenager affection. The dad knew that meant touching. When children are small, we can show them that physical affection by cuddling and holding them. When they grow up, they don't lose the need for such demonstrations. Though a father may not be able to hold his teenage daughter on his lap, or a mother cuddle her sixteen-year-old son, it's important for parents to find age- and gender-appropriate means of showing affection physically.

THE FOUR PHASES OF A CHILD'S DEVELOPMENT

Participative parents know how to express love and communicate with their growing kids because they understand the stages of their children's development. I don't profess to have a specialty degree in child development, but I have a "degree" in the most demanding university of all—the school of front-line, in-the-trenches parenting. Through that experience, I noted four main phases of development. Jo Beth and I learned we had to adjust our parenting style to the phase through which a particular child was passing.

The Care-Giving Phase

The first is the *care-giving phase,* which ranges from birth to about two years old. This is full-time, all-consuming parenting. Bottles, diapers, naps, scampering to the doctor's office, and loud wails in the night are part of this phase. At this point, your whole life is defined by the precious gift God has given you. You are the caregiver, and the child is 100 percent dependent on you.

The Authority Phase

Next is the *authority phase,* spanning ages two to six years. Now the parent begins to assert leadership. The little one gets its first inklings that mom and dad call the shots. The child in this phase will test the limits. He or she has all kinds of strategies for doing that—from temper tantrums to sticking fingers in forbidden places, such as electrical sockets. Permissive parents have a one-dimensional vision that believes the home is always a pure democracy. Not so, and this is the stage where the participative parent will let the little one know the father and mother have the authority and leadership.

The Teaching and Training Phase

Third is the *teaching and training phase,* spanning ages six to twelve. Meaningful discipline enters at this phase. Up to now, discipline has been administered to stop harmful activities. Now, parents begin to connect discipline with reasons and purposes, so the child will understand why he got a time-out or a spanking. Parents must discipline with discernment by understanding the situation and the child. Then, appropriate discipline can be administered. This discernment will guide the mom or dad in selecting the disciplinary method.

Parents can learn to communicate effectively with their children by studying Jesus' style. He loved to teach in parables. Through life experiences, even the simplest person could understand His truths—though often the complex religious types couldn't!

One dad I heard about really caught on to the parable principle. He took his son fishing in New Hampshire. Late that night, the boy caught the biggest bass he had ever seen. The father glanced at his watch. "Son," he said, sadly, "in New Hampshire there are seasons for catching certain kinds of fish, and bass season doesn't start for another two hours. We're gonna have to put this big fish back." The boy protested, but with love and understanding, the dad replied, "That's the law; we have to put it back in the water."

Years later, as an architect in New York City, the son remembered the bass. Every time he was tempted to bend the rules, yield to temptation, cheat a customer, or take a shortcut that might harm someone else, the man thought of the lesson of noncompromise he had learned from his father. That bass, he knew, was definitely the catch of a lifetime!

The Coaching-Cheerleading Phase

The fourth developmental stage is the *coaching or cheerleading phase,* from ages twelve to nineteen years. Our offspring venture out into the real game of life at this point, and we parents are on the sidelines. We call the plays from our watching position, but sometimes the kids out on the field call their own. If you've done the right job through the earlier phases, your children will heed your coaching. If you've been proactive, godly, and sensitive at the other stages, they will listen now, even if they have to focus their ears to hear your voice over the crowd.

When the son or daughter crosses the threshold at about nineteen, you transition from being a coach to a trusted friend. Before, you were looking down from above and had to make special efforts to get down to their level. But now it's eye-to-eye, over a cup of coffee or in some other friendship setting. Parental leadership at this point doesn't come through authority but relationship. That's the goal for the parent-child interaction.

Dr. Phil Littleford and his twelve-year-old son went fishing in Alaska. They boarded a little pontoon plane to take them to various places to fish. Joining them on the fishing expedition were the pilot and another fisherman.

The small group flew to a remote lake and began to fish, but they failed to catch anything the entire day. The next day the pilot flew them to another spot in the arctic region. The pilot spotted salmon coming in and was certain Littleford, his son, and the other man would catch fish. As soon as they dropped their lines into the water, the fish were practically tackling each other to get on the hook.

At the end of the day, when the foursome went to the plane to take off for base camp, they discovered the tide had washed the plane up onto the rocks. They couldn't take off, so the group decided to spend the night. They cooked fish and had a glorious night in the pristine environment.

The next morning they awoke, and the tide had come back in. The group broke camp, loaded back into the little pontoon plane and took off. However, they discovered too late that one of the pontoons had been cracked by the rocks and had filled with water. The plane began to gyrate as it rose, then plummeted back into the icy water.

All four survived the crash. The pilot and the other man swam for shore and made it. Dr. Littleford and his son, Mark, dived in and headed for dry land. Dr. Littleford was a strong swimmer and could make it to shore easily, but Mark was struggling to swim against the riptide. The two men on the shore watched Dr. Littleford swim back for his son. There was no way the father could swim and pull the boy against the strong tides, so the father just held his boy. Slowly, they were carried away by the current. Eventually the two disappeared altogether over the horizon. Both father and son died shortly thereafter of hypothermia.[3]

When I first read this story, I thought, "What would I have done if I were that father?" Though I'm not the heroic type, I decided 100 percent I would have stayed with my boys. I don't think that's anything particularly heroic or unusual. Most, if not all parents, would have done the same thing.

PARENTING MEANS SACRIFICE

If you would be willing to die for your children, are you willing to do what it takes to build the right stuff into their lives as they are growing up? It will mean you must make the sacrifice of yourself and your life. It's those daily sacrifices that build a man out of your son and a woman out of your daughter. If you make this sacrifice, your children will grow up to be God-fearing adults, and they will rise up and call you blessed (see Proverbs 20:7; 31:28–30).

Passive parents practice laissez-faire parenting and are reluctant to pay the high price of involvement.

Possessive parents practice parenting by law and are often unwilling to make the sacrifices of genuine relationship.

Participative parents practice parenting by grace. They know it took the Cross to win grace for humanity. They are willing to "take up their cross" and follow Christ in extending the elements of grace—love, patience, endurance—to their children.

QUESTIONS FOR PARENTS

1. Would you classify your parenting style as passive, possessive, or participative?

2. How would your children classify you?

3. In what areas in the lives of each of your children do they need your affirmation?

4. Under what kind of circumstances should a parent intervene in a child's life, and when should the parent pull back?

A FINAL WORD: A PARENT'S PROUDEST MOMENT

One of life's prouder moments for a parent is to have a child choose to follow in his footsteps. Please don't misunderstand—I would be proud of my sons in any vocational endeavor. But it is especially thrilling for Jo Beth and me to see all three of our boys in full-time Christian ministry. I'll never forget Ed and Ben's first sermons or Cliff's first concert. They have a very proud man as their dad!

As Americans, we all were able to observe another father's proudest moment as a son followed in his footsteps. On January 21, 2000, George Walker Bush took the oath of office to become the 43rd president of the United States of America. There were parades, dinners, and dances into the night. At seemingly every turn President Bush was met with handshakes, well wishes, photographers, and news crews. All in all, it was an exhausting day for everyone involved, especially the new president and his family.

Present that day was the 41st president of the United States,

George Herbert Walker Bush. The former president and his wife, Barbara, took in every detail of their son's inauguration. The television cameras caught the proud parents every chance they could.

The day was chilly and damp for those who gathered at the nation's capital. Jo Beth and I were honored to attend the swearing-in ceremony. We can only imagine what a thrilling and emotional moment it must have been the first time the two presidents entered the Oval Office together. Former President Bush had sacrificed years of his life for his country in that room. He knew all too well what was ahead for his son. Certainly America's newest president was proud to have his dad with him as he took his first steps into the unique chapter he would contribute to his family's legacy and his nation's history.

This is parenting's proudest moment—when we see that our kids are okay. That they're going to make it in life. And they will, if we apply the ten commandments of parenting. When we get it right, moms and dads, we'll have healthy families and a healthy nation. Better yet, we'll make a difference for all eternity!

NOTES

Introduction

1. Gilda Radner, *It's Always Something* (San Francisco: HarperCollins, 2000), 237. The dog actually belonged to the cousin of Gilda's childhood nanny; the comedienne also told the story during a network TV interview program.
2. David Blankenhorn, *Fatherless America* (New York: HarperCollins, 1995), 177.
3. Saint Augustine, *Confessions* (New York: Barnes and Noble Books, 1992), 192.
4. "President Bush Receives IBS' Bilingual Bible," IBS World News press release, 16 May 2003, Colorado Springs: International Bible Society.

Commandment 1: Thou Shalt Build a Functional Family

1. As quoted in "After 9/11: Mending the Broken Hearth," *Family Times* newsletter, September/October 2002, vol. 14, no. 5. Accessed 23 September 2003 at http://www.familiesnorthwest.org/familytimes.cfm.
2. Edna Gundersen, Bill Keveney, and Ann Oldenburg, "'The Osbournes' Popular in America's Living Rooms," *USA Today*, 19 April 2002.
3. Ibid.
4. William J. Bennett, *The Index of Leading Cultural Indicators*, rev. ed. (Colorado Springs: Waterbrook, 2000), 14.
5. Vox Day, "Breaking Little Hearts," 17 March 2003. Accessed 23 September 2003 at http://www.worldnetdaily.com/news/article.asp?article_ID= 31554.
6. Bennett, *The Index of Leading Cultural Indicators*, 14.
7. Charles Wesley, "O for a Thousand Tongues to Sing." In public domain.

Commandment 2: Thou Shalt Love Thy Children

1. At age eighty-six, Abraham had his first son, but this child was born of his handmaiden, not by his wife Sarai, who God promised would bear the promised son (see Genesis 17:15–19).
2. James C. Dobson, *Complete Family and Home Reference Guide* (Carol Stream, Ill.: Tyndale, 2000). Accessed 10 September 2003 at www.family.org/docstudy/solid/a0003519.html.
3. James S. Hewett, *Illustrations Unlimited* (Wheaton, Ill.: Tyndale, 1988), 195.

Commandment 3: Thou Shalt Model Godliness

1. Plato, *The Republic: Book II*. Cited in www.classicreader.com/read.php/sid.8/bookid.1788/sec.22/cached.
2. David Lowenthal, "The Case for Censorship." Accessed 5 August 2003 at www.jewishworldreview.com/ weekly/standard082099.asp.
3. "Study Finds Parental Influence Still Important During Adolescence." Accessed 5 August 2003 at www.acs.ohio-state.edu/units/research/archive/adoldel.htm.
4. "Teens Report Peer Pressure to have Sex," Associated Press, 20 May 2003.
5. Stephen L. Carter, *The Culture of Disbelief* (New York: HarperCollins, 1993), 183–84.
6. Carl Pickhardt, "Keeping Parental Influence in Perspective."Accessed 5 August 2003 at www.carlpickhardt.com.
7. "Report: Jack Osbourne Checks into Rehab," Associated Press, April 29, 2003.

Commandment 4: Thou Shalt Teach Thy Children

1. Paul Woodruff, *Reverence: Renewing a Forgotten Virtue* (Oxford, England: Oxford Univ. Press, 2001), 67.
2. Accessed 8 September, 2003 at www.butlerwebs.com/jokes/parents.htm.
3. Cited in Robert Bork, *Slouching Towards Gomorrah* (New York: HarperCollins, 1996), 23.
4. David Wallechinsky, *The Complete Book of the Olympics* (London: Aurum Press, 1996), as cited in David Wallechinsky, "The 1936 Olympics—and a Friendship," *Friday Morning Story, September 22, 2000.* Accessed 23 September 2003 at www.52best.com/ stories/jesse.asp.

Commandment 5: Thou Shalt Spend Time With Thy Children

1. John Trent, "Be There!" *Focus on the Family,* October 2000, 7.

Commandment 6: Thou Shalt Discipline Thy Children

1. Liza Porteus, "Experts: 'Buddy' Parents No Friends to Kids," *Fox News,* 13 May 2003.
2. Ibid.
3. Professor Diane Baumrind of the University of California, Berkeley, identified and described some of the parenting styles that will be cited here. E.E. Maccoby, J. A. Martin, and other experts have updated descriptions of the styles.

4. George Brackman, "Parenting Isn't for Cowards." Accessed 9 September 2003 at www.lighthousehealingministries.com/parentingcowards.htm.

5. Nancy Darling, "Parenting Style and Its Correlates," *ERIC Digests* (Champagne, Ill.: Clearinghouse on Elementary and Early Childhood Education (ERIC), 1999), 1.

6. Ibid.

7. Ibid.

8. As cited in "Not Guilty Plea"; accessed 24 September 2003 at www.abcnews. go.com/sections/GMA/GoodMorningAmerica/GMA020923Mother_beating_ interview.html.

9. John Derbyshire, "The Life! How will my kids turn out?" *National Review Online* 28 April 2003. Accessed 10 September 2003 at www.nationalreview.com/ derbyshire/derbyshire42803.asp .

10. Patricia McBroom, "UC Berkeley study finds no lasting harm among adolescents from moderate spanking earlier in childhood," UC Berkeley News Release, August 24, 2001.

11. Ibid.

12. Diana Baumrind, "The Short and Long Term Consequences of Corporal Punishment," *Pediatrics* 98, no. 4 (October 1996).

Commandment 7: Thou Shalt Encourage Thy Children

1. *Theological Dictionary of the New Testament*, ed. Gerhard Kittel, vol. 1 (Grand Rapids: Eerdmans, 1964), 37.

2. John Haggai, *My Son Johnny,* (Atlanta: Kobrey Press, 1978), 12.

3. Mary Ann Zehr, "Foreign Teens Say Academics Given More Priority Back Home," *Education Week*, September 12, 2001.

4. Walter E. Williams, "Asian excellence, American mediocrity," *WorldNetDaily,* 16 June 1999. Accessed 24 September 2003 at www.asianam.org/universities _against_asians.htm.

5. V. Dion Haynes, "Dueling Experts See Grade Inflation As Crisis, Canard," *Chicago Tribune*, 2 January 2003, 8.

6. Kirk Douglas, *The Ragman's Son* (New York: The Free Press, 1994), 88–89.

Commandment 8: Thou Shalt Provide Stability and Security for Thy Children

1. C. F. Keil and F. Delitzsch, *Commentary on the Old Testament*, vol. 3 (Grand Rapids: Eerdmans, 1983), 103.

2. *The Westminster Dictionary of the Bible*, ed. John D. Davis and Henry Snyder Gehman (Philadelphia: Westminster, 1944), 77.

3. Saint Augustine, *Confessions*, trans. R. S. Pine-Coffin (New York: Barnes and Noble, 1992), 192.

Commandment 9: Thou Shalt Have the Sex Talk with Thy Children

1. Robert E. Rector, Kirk A. Johnson, and Lauren R. Noyes, "Sexually Active Teenagers Are More Likely to Be Depressed and to Attempt Suicide," *Center*

for Data Analysis Report #03-04 (Washington, D. C.: The Heritage Foundation), 3 June 2003.

2. Jan Fountain, "Sex in the Media." Accessed 10 September 2003 at www.umkc. edu/sites/ hsw/other/sexmedia.html.

3. "Children Learn Sex from TV, Says ATL," press release of the [British] Association of Teachers and Lecturers, 6 April 2001. Accessed on 10 September 2003 at http://www.askatl.org.uk/news/press releases/2001/apr2001/P pn010406 2.htm.

4. Fountain, "Sex in the Media."

5. Catherine Donaldson-Evans, "Teen Mags Tackle Sex," *Fox News,* 5 June 2003.

6. As quoted in "Children Learn Sex from TV, Says ATL," press release, 6 April 2001. Ferguson is president of the Association of Teachers and Lecturers, a professional organization representing teachers and support staff in England, Wales, and Northern Ireland.

7. Alexander Marks, "More Teens Have Sex and Fewer Parents Know," *The Christian Science Monitor,* 9 June 2003.

8. Ibid.

9. Robert E. Rector, "The Effectiveness of Abstinence Education Programs in Reducing Sexual Activity Among Youth," Backgrounder #1533, 8 April 2002. Accessed 12 September 2003 at www.Heritage.org/research/family/ BG1533. cfm.

10. Ibid.

11. Barbara Brake, "AIDS/HIV Rate Slashed in Uganda After 10 Years of True Love Waits," Baptist Press news report, Executive Committee of the Southern Baptist Convention, 25 February 2003.

12. Ed Young, *Pure Sex* (Sisters, Ore.: Multnomah, 1997).

Commandment 10: Thou Shalt Not Be a Passive Parent

1. Lee Teng-hui, *The Road to Democracy* (Tokyo: PHP Institute Inc., 1999), 42.

2. John A. Hutchison, *Paths of Faith* (New York: McGraw-Hill, 1969), 631.

3. Patrick M. Morley, *The Man in the Mirror* (Grand Rapids: Zondervan, 1997), 105.

Marriage is God's idea. He planned it. He designed it.
And if you follow His blueprint, it will be more rewarding,
more loving, more exciting than you ever imagined.

ISBN: 0-8024-3146-1

In words that are profound, often humorous, but always biblical, Ed Young draws from decades of counseling couples to provide 10 Commandments for a lifelong marriage that sizzles. God wants your marriage to be nothing short of incredible. And it could all begin with this amazing book.

For more information contact
www.winningwalk.org or www.second.org

Call me picky but I buy a message much quicker when it is propped up by the real thing behind the billboard. I like a public persona that's not a misfit to its private side. This man and his message fit. The Ten Commandments of Marriage *not only tells you "what." Thankfully, it tells you "how." Ed Young has taken the principles of Scripture and has had the courage to test them on the linoleum glued to average life on Planet Earth.*
Beth Moore, Author and speaker

MOODY
PUBLISHERS
THE NAME YOU CAN TRUST.

1-800-678-6928 www.MoodyPublishers.org

THE 10 COMMANDMENTS OF PARENTING TEAM

ACQUIRING EDITOR:
Mark Tobey

COPY EDITOR:
Jim Vincent

BACK COVER COPY:
The Smartt Guys

COVER DESIGN:
The Smartt Guys

INTERIOR DESIGN:
Ragont Design

PRINTING AND BINDING:
Quebecor World Book Services

The typeface for the text of this book is
New Aster